Arvin Vohra

MATERIALISTIC MINIMALISM

2017

Published and distributed by
Roland Media Distribution
www.RMDGlobal.net

Edited by Chelsey M. Snyder

Cover Design by Kostis Pavlou
Typesetting by Art Biro Network

ISBN: 978-0-9801446-8-0

ARVIN VOHRA

Materialistic **MINIMALISM**

CONTENTS

Materialistic Minimalism

More is better.

That is what advertisers, manufacturers, and brands have been telling us forever.
But more isn't better. Better is better.

More is better works for money. It's better to have a billion dollars than twenty dollars. But it doesn't work for things. A billion pairs of socks aren't better than twenty. A billion Armani suits wouldn't fit in your closet – or in all the closets of everyone you've ever met combined. A billion grass fed steaks would spoil long before you could eat them, and become a billion mold and bacteria farms.

Much like you, I have no desire to live as an ascetic monk. I like material things as much as the next guy. To be frank, I probably like material things about 100 times as much as the next guy.

Like most people, I spend part of my time thinking about philosophy, religion, and spirituality. But, also like most people, I spend a lot more time browsing online for things I'd like to buy. And of course, along with countless others, I spent a lot of my life believing that more and more things improve your life.

The problem with "more is better" is not that it's overly greedy or materialistic. The problem is that it is not a particularly effective way to be materialistic.

This book is not about eschewing material things in favor of spiritual pursuits. There are plenty of books on that subject already. The Old Testament, the New Testament, the Koran, the Bhagavad Gita, the Dhammapada, the Tao Te Ching are some of the more famous ones.

This book is not about being less materialistic; it's about being more materialistic.

Most people are amateurs at being materialistic. This book can help make you a pro. And like all pros, you will start using vastly different methods from amateurs. It's not enough to do more of what amateurs do; you must learn to do something qualitatively better.

Materialistic Minimalism has improved many parts of my life, saved me money, and even helped me learn about luxuries I would never otherwise have discovered. It has also created a more peaceful home environment for me, made it easier to handle stress calmly and effectively, and made travel a relaxed and easy process. I hope to take you on a similar journey to my own, with similar benefits.

A Little About Me

My academic background is in economics, and I worked as an actuary for a while. The ideas in Materialistic Minimalism, however, come much more from the work that I currently do (although the economics background certainly helps).

For over a decade, I have worked as a private tutor with many wealthy clients. Through those close relationships, I have seen good and bad ways to be materialistic. I've seen and learned from so many mistakes (many of which I have personally made). I have also seen and learned of techniques that work.

I've shared the methods of Materialistic Minimalism with friends and family. Some have cherry picked particular techniques and ideas. Others have adopted all parts of Materialistic Minimalism. People in both groups have benefited.

From a technical standpoint, it's pretty easy. There are some principles to understand, and a few tips and tricks that are useful. But psychologically, Materialistic Minimalism is hard. You have to fight all kinds of compulsions and psychological blocks. At first, it's really, really hard.

But it's also really worth it. They say fortune favors the bold. If you make this bold move toward Materialistic Minimalism, you can save money, own things worth having, and be happier.

CHAPTER 1:
The Problem of Scarcity

The human species evolved in scarcity. There was always a danger of running out of food, not having shelter, etc.

Biologically, that's why we store fat so easily. Fat is stored energy; when you have no food, your body can get energy from the fat in order to keep going. It's also why we are attracted to high fat, sugary foods that make us fat. For most of human evolution, getting enough food was a challenge. Getting enough calories was hard. Thus, it made biological sense for us to be drawn to high calorie foods, rather than low calorie foods. An early human who didn't like high calorie foods would have run out of energy.

But in the modern age, those instincts are less useful. We have essentially infinite access to high calorie foods. If we follow our instincts and eat only high sugar, high fat food, that would present a major health danger. Even now, heart disease is the number one killer of Americans.

Until the recent past, humans have also lived in a time of scarcity of things. I don't mean that people didn't have enough fancy things; I mean people didn't have enough anything. They didn't have enough clothes, shoes, tools, etc.

Because of that, humans developed cultures of saving and protecting the things that they own. We are taught to save and cherish our possessions from an early age, and we are chastised when we abandon things or ruin them. We know that we should never lose or break our things, or randomly give them away. We are told to save things, even things we don't need right away, since we might need them later. As the old saying goes, "Waste not, want not!"

These rules worked for thousands of years. They were part of almost every culture on earth. They made sense.

But they don't make sense anymore. Today, in the first world, that scarcity is gone. Very few people will say they don't have enough clothes. Sure, a person may not have enough clothes that he likes. There may be a specific item of clothing that he cannot afford. But even lower middle class people rarely run entirely out of clothes.

Your Inner Hoarder

Chances are, you don't currently face raw scarcity. You are not in danger of running out of clothes or food. But there's a good chance you're acting like it.

Those compulsions that kept the human race alive for thousands of years are still part of your psyche.

Even if, right now, you walk over to your closet, and find your least favorite shirt, pants, or scarf, you will feel weird about just giving it away. It may be something you have not worn in a year. It's adding nothing to your life at all. In fact, it's detracting from your life by taking up space. But if you reach for it right now to put it into a bag for donation, or just to leave it by the side of the road for someone else to pick up, you will feel something stopping you.

That something is your Inner Hoarder, and it is clever. It has helped the human race survive for thousands of years. It has plenty of experience stopping people from getting rid of unwanted things.

When you reach for an unwanted object to give away, your Inner Hoarder immediately starts trying to convince you to stop. Right away, it will say: "Wait! You might need it later." It will then come up with some elaborate and unlikely circumstance in which you will need it.

For example: "Sure, you hate that shirt. But what if you decide to paint the ceiling next year? You'll want to wear a shirt you don't like, so you can get paint on it. You have to keep the shirt!"

And usually that's enough for the Inner Hoarder to stop you. Unfortunately for you, it has genetics and culture on its side.

But what happens if you push harder? What if you say, "That's idiotic, I'm not painting the ceiling next year or ever"? And you keep on reaching to donate that junk in your closet that you clearly do not want?

The Inner Hoarder reaches deeper into its bag of tricks. Maybe it says, "Wait! That shirt has some technical market value. You should sell it. Put an ad on craigslist and eBay, and sell it. Maybe you'll get a dollar or two. Waste not, want not!"

That's one of the Inner Hoarder's dirty tricks. It gives you a choice between spending hours selling a 2 dollar shirt, then mailing it out, and then doing a bunch of other annoying things, or just giving up and keeping the stupid thing. Obviously, you keep the shirt.

The Inner Hoarder is a worthy adversary. It has many, many tricks up its sleeve.

You try to donate the most hideously ugly sweater you own, and the Inner Hoarder says, "Wait! That was a gift from your grandmother. Don't you love your grandmother? Who knows how long she'll be alive. Do you want to lose your connection to her?"

Reeling with guilt, you put the sweater back, and continue to never wear it.

You try to donate something that you bought yourself, but just don't like, and the Inner Hoarder says, "Wait! Think about how hard you worked to be able to pay for that. You've already spent so much money on it. Shouldn't you at least keep it?"

Embarrassed by your poor decision making, you give up, put the item back, and slink away. Obviously, you couldn't be trusted to make the right decision when you bought it. How can you be trusted to make the right decision now?

The Inner Hoarder can always find your most vulnerable emotional pressure points and hit you there. You reach for an ugly, uncomfortable scarf to donate, and the Inner Hoarder reaches deep into its bag of insane reasons to keep everything: "Wait! What kind of person are you who will reject something just for being ugly? Haven't you ever felt rejected? Didn't you hate it when your teacher/parent/coach/grandparent showed favoritism to so-and-so? And now you're going to do the same to this poor, humble scarf."

On the verge of tears, you apologize to the scarf, and promise to keep it forever.

The Inner Hoarder is ruthless and devious. It has many disguises. Learning to outsmart it will both make you smarter and put you back in charge. You'll be able to make decisions that improve your life, and even improve the lives of others.

In later parts of this book, we'll talk about how to battle the Inner Hoarder directly. But we aren't there yet. First, we'll explore some of the simple techniques that will immediately start to improve your daily life.

CHAPTER 2:
Every Day is Special

Special Occasions

Have you ever gone to an estate sale? At these sales of the belongings of the recently deceased, you can get fascinating insights into people's lives and habits.

One thing you'll often see at estate sales: fancy things that have barely been used. Elegant wallets and purses, fancy pens, glasses and silverware for special occasions. Beautiful objects that people had been saving for special occasions.

In fairness, they probably used those things for some special occasions. But the fact is, many people clearly could have used those special occasion things a lot more often.

It's a major part of the mindset of most of us: we only use nice things on special occasions. It's part of what makes them feel special. We say, "This is the outfit I wear on special days," and that makes a particular day feel more special.

Sometimes, there is a kind of engineering logic to it as well. We say, "this dress/jacket/etc. is made out of a delicate material. I can wear it at most 5 times in my life. So, I should wear it at my wedding, at my kids' weddings, and at 2 other special occasions."

But often, there is no engineering logic at all, only sentimentality. Many of the things we save for special occasions are essentially indestructible. A nice bracelet or watch may be made out of diamonds and platinum. Unless your daily routine involves nuclear war or journeys into center of the sun, nothing is likely to damage it.

The idea of saving nice things for special occasions affects our daily habits. Suppose you're about to head over to the grocery store. Do you grab nice jeans or sweatpants? Your wool coat or a sweatshirt and camping vest? A nice t-shirt or a ratty one? Most of us instinctively reach for something ratty, something "casual". We're saving the nice things for a more special part of the week.

That approach is common and emotionally familiar. It feels natural to wear costume jewelry most of the time, and real jewelry once a year. We find comfort in wearing ratty and unattractive t-shirts most of the time, and nice blouses, shirts, or even nicer t-shirts only on important days. We don't question the use of our junky silverware every day, while we save the nice silverware for a once a year affair.

The alternative, using only our best things all the time, seems almost completely insane. It feels spoiled, arrogant, wasteful, and ungrateful. You might have special occasion silverware, but if you use it every day, wouldn't that make you some kind of irresponsible degenerate? You might have a nice pen you received as a gift, but using such a thing daily would be disrespecting the preciousness of the gift, right? Doesn't wearing your more expensive, real jewelry every day, mean you're acting like some spoiled brat?

Saving nice things for special occasions feels safe and correct. But does it have an actual advantage over the alternative? Are you better off saving nice things for special days, or using them all the time?

It's hard to think critically about this question. You have a lifetime of experience that says, "save the nice stuff for special occasions only." The Inner Hoarder also supports that. If you start using your nicest things all the time, then you obviously wouldn't need all the junk piled up in your closet. You might donate the junk, an act which the archaic Inner Hoarder perceives as a threat to survival.

The Hypotheticals

So, let's imagine a very different situation. Suppose you're going on a one week vacation to a Caribbean island. When you get to the hotel, they tell you that they've accidentally given you two rooms. You won't be charged any additional money, but you get to keep both rooms for a week.

The first room is perfectly nice. The bed is nice, the shower is fine, the lighting is fine. There is nothing wrong with it.

The second room is palatial. The bed is phenomenal, the shower has fancy massage settings, the windows give majestic views of the ocean. The TV is huge.

What do you do? You have both rooms; where do you sleep?

You can alternate every night. You can stay in one room the entire time.

You could stay in the average room for 6 days, and then spend one special day in the palatial room. You could do the reverse.

Of course, most people will stay the entire time in the palatial room. Why on earth would you choose to lower your standard of living?

What if the same thing happened for a month? Most people would stay in the nice room the entire time.

The same would be true for a year. Or for ten years. Or an entire lifetime. If you had both rooms, but could only be in one room each day, almost everyone would choose to be in the nice room every single day. You wouldn't artificially lower your standard of living for even a single hour. You might never even set foot in the lesser room.

Suppose you win a contest. As a prize, you can wear one of two bracelets for a day. One is a rare, fancy emerald bracelet. The other is a 10 cent, ugly, uncomfortable plastic bracelet. What do you choose?

Most people choose the emerald bracelet.

What if the rule is this: for the rest of your life, you can pick either the fancy bracelet or the junky bracelet at the beginning of each day.

In this case, most people would choose the nice bracelet every single day.

We can do the same thought experiment with shirts, accessories, shoes, tools, cars, silverware, or pens. Almost everyone will choose to use the nicer thing almost every single day.

Consider how completely different from usual behavior that is. In our own lives, we wear the nice bracelet rarely, and the junky bracelet daily. But in this imaginary world, when given a choice, we always choose the nice bracelet, and almost never the junky bracelet.

That's not an easy thing to reconcile. How can those diametrically opposite instincts both be a part of you? Why, in real life, do we rarely use the nicer thing? Why, in this thought experiment, do we always use the nicer thing?

Objectively, it seems to make sense to always use

the nice thing. You get more enjoyment out of fancier, higher quality things.

In fact, from a purely objective sense, the "special occasions" approach makes absolutely no economic sense at all. It basically involves artificially lowering your standard of living 364 days out of the year just to make the last day seem good.

It would be like eating moldy mayonnaise 364 days a year, and then normal food one day a year, in order to make that one day seem special. Or sitting on the floor 364 days a year, and using a chair one day a year, to help raise that day above the rest. Or taking cold water showers 364 days a year, and then a hot water shower one day a year, reminding you how glorious only that one day is.

Compulsion

When behavior doesn't make rational sense, it's often a good idea to consider that it might be a psychological compulsion. This particular psychological compulsion, like many others, often comes from childhood.

During the early phases of my education business, I did a lot of in-home tutoring. I got the chance to observe kids of many cultures at many ages in their home environments. I noticed this: roughly 100% of kids want to use the best things available 100% of the time. Every teenager wants to drive his parent's nicest car. Every kid wants to use the nicest TV and game system. Even infants want to chew on the nicest cell phone or remote control.

Kids that are very intensively taught manners seek out the most superior things, of course. But even those kids, before they were taught etiquette, always sought the best.

The problem: kids love to lose and break things. So, parents try to keep kids away from nicer things. They say that the nice things are for special occasions, purely to keep them away from kids.

The natural instinct is to exclusively use the best of everything. There is no innate desire to use low quality garbage, or even to use second rate things. When the 5th generation of a thing comes out, no child is begging for the older, 1st generation product.

There is certainly no desire to avoid all nice things in order to then later use the nice things, making that later day special. That compulsion is purely external, and requires years of training to convince kids to follow along.

The closest natural inclination that I have seen involves food, and it is important to understand how that natural inclination differs from the compulsion to avoid using nice things.

Many kids will save the best part of their meal for last.

Why is that different? Because when you eat a meal, it is gone. If you eat your french fries first, then they are no longer available. So, if you want your last taste memory to be of french fries, you must save them until the end of the meal.

But if you use nice silverware, it does not vanish. When you wear a nice bracelet once, it doesn't become unusable.

Saving a nice bottle of champagne for the end of the week makes sense. You can only drink it once. But saving a nice bracelet for a special day does not make the same kind of sense. You can wear that bracelet every single day without using it up.

The Junk Moat

Many people have a few prized possessions that they literally never use. For some, it is a pen or piece of jewelry received as a gift. For others, it is an expensive pair of shoes or item of clothing that they bought and are waiting for the right occasion to use.

To stop ourselves from using that amazing thing, we surround it with junky alternatives. This "junk moat" blocks us from ever reaching the high-quality thing.

For example, to block yourself from using the nice pen you received as a graduation gift, you may have an entire drawer full of five cent pens. Many of them you may have gotten for free as part of some promotional giveaway. There may be literally hundreds of them, ensuring that you'll never have an excuse to use the good pen.

You might have some exquisite sterling silverware. But to make sure you never actually use it, you have several sets of low grade flatware. That ensures that you'll never have an excuse to use the good silverware (except, perhaps, once a year).

The same is true of shoes, clothes, and even food. Junk moats surround everything good.

Junk moats do two things. First, they lower our standards of living. We could be using nice things. Instead, we end up using junk. Second, they create clutter. They fill up our homes with garbage. Sometimes, junk moats get so big that we cannot even find the nice things!

Soon, we're going to talk about draining some of those junk moats, and taking some initial steps in improving your standard of living.

CHAPTER 3:
Not Using is Not Having

Suppose you have a really nice pen sitting in a safe place in your closet, carefully hidden away. It sits there for decades. You never use it for your entire life.

How is that different from just not having the pen?

In some sentimental way, you can take a kind of abstract comfort in knowing the pen exists. But a pen adds more value to our lives when it's used as a pen, rather than as a metaphysical security blanket.

When you refuse to use that pen, you are keeping its value as an abstraction, but losing its value as a pen. In other words, you are throwing out the pragmatic aspects of the pen. Because of your behavior, the pen is just something that takes up space, rather than something that improves your life.

When you have something nice, but never use it, it's a lot like just throwing it away. It's wasting the great thing. It's like managing a sports team, and keeping the best player on the bench. It's like managing a business, and never having your smartest people do anything.

If you buy or receive expensive food, and then refuse to eat it, you're obviously wasting the food. If you wait for the food to become completely rotten and unusable, it's obvious that you're being wasteful.

With non-perishable objects like pens and jewelry, most people don't wait for the object to decay. After all, a metal pen can last for thousands of years. Instead, they wait for themselves to die of old age.

It's equivalently wasteful, albeit turned around a bit. You have an amazing object. You refuse to ever use it. What could possibly be more wasteful?

Saving for Posterity

Sometimes we try to rationalize this wastefulness by convincing ourselves that we are saving the nice object for the next generation. In other words, we aren't just keeping a nice pen and never using it because we are wasteful lunatics. We are preserving an heirloom for the next generation.

To some extent, it's a nice idea. There is something sweet about passing a prized object from parent to child. A great grandparent's wedding ring connects us deeply to a family legacy.

But passing down three hundred objects doesn't work the same. I've been to enough estate sales to tell exactly what happens to those prized possessions that people save for the next generation: they get sold for a few dollars to strangers.

Your kids and grandkids may not even have the same preferences as you. Fashions may change so much that the initial object becomes unusable forty years from now. Today, a fur coat is a luxurious status symbol. Fifty years from now, it may be seen as grotesque and barbaric.

I've spoken to many people about the heirlooms they most treasure. It's always the things that their parents or grandparents used the most. "My father kept this on his desk and used it constantly. When I use it, it reminds me of him." "My grandmother wore these earrings every day. When I wear them, I feel close to her." "My grandfather wore this watch daily. When I wear it, I think of our best times together."

Here's what I have never heard: "It's some pen that I think my grandmother kept in her closet. I never saw her use it ever. I have no association with my grandmother at all when I use it, since I had no idea she even had it or liked it. But when I use this pen, I feel soooo close to her." That would be preposterous.

The fact is, if you do your job right, your kids and grandkids may be able to afford things you can't even dream about. I am fortunate to make much more money than my grandfather did. I keep his ring, not because it has some particularly high monetary value, but because I never saw him without it.

The heirlooms that matter will be the ones you use, not the ones you don't use. If you want your descendants to cherish that special object the way you cherish it, you have to actually cherish it your-self, by using it.

CHAPTER 4:
Your First Exercise

As you've seen in the first few chapters (and perhaps in your own life) most people use their low-quality items, and refuse to use their high-quality items. In doing so, we end up wasting our nicer things. We artificially lower our standards of living. We surround themselves with low grade junk.

Without spending a single cent, we all could improve our lives. It would be as simple as using the better things we already own, and refusing to use low quality junk. But compulsions prevent us all from doing so.

In my case, it took me a long time to realize I was doing that. Once I realized what I was doing, I initially tried to just force myself to use my nicer things. It worked about half the time, but the natural compulsion to use lower quality things in order to preserve higher quality items was sometimes just too difficult to overcome. If I was tired or in a rush, I would immediately default to lower quality things.

So, I decided to take that option away. I grabbed a grocery bag, stuffed a few of my rattiest, ugliest, and most ill-fitting t-shirts into it, and donated them to Goodwill.

The change was surprisingly significant. Now that I simply could not wear those t-shirts, my minimum standard of appearance was higher. Even at my laziest, I looked more presentable.

It was a tiny change. I donated maybe five t-shirts out of over a hundred. But it was the first step. That tiny step was the beginning of Materialistic Minimalism.

Over the next months, I continued that process. I donated one bag after another of lower quality things. Each time I did so, my appearance improved. I couldn't wear an unattractive shirt because I just didn't have any. I couldn't wear an ill-fitting sweater because I no longer owned one. No matter how tired I was or what kind of mood I was in, I couldn't drop below a certain threshold of wardrobe quality.

It was quite similar to what many people do with food. They remove all junk food from their homes, making it impossible to randomly binge on junk food at 3 a.m. I did the same thing with junk clothes. Then with junk shoes. I took them out of my house so I simply could not use them.

Your First Step

So now I invite you to take that first step. Grab a bag. A small bag is fine. Put at least one item of clothing to donate into it. It can be a ratty, old shirt. It can be a sweater that doesn't fit quite right. It can be your least favorite scarf, or a pair of unflattering or uncomfortable jeans. Anything.

If you live in a busy city, you can just leave it on the sidewalk with a sign that says, "Free". If you don't, then just look up the nearest Goodwill or Salvation Army drop off location, or wait for a nearby church to do a clothing drive (this happens quite often). Some charity groups will even come to your house to pick up your donations.

If you managed to achieve that: congratulations. You've won your first battle against your Inner Hoarder. You've taken a first step into a better life.

If you did not: that's okay too. Sometimes, it takes a few tries before you can make that first step. It may be a little harder for you than for other people. Maybe you grew up in a very strict and frugal household. The compulsion against donating old clothes may be stronger in you than it is in other people. But once you can overcome that, it also means that the strength of your character will increase more. You will gain more psychological discipline than other people might. You may actually be confronting a full-blown phobia. Those who have learned to overcome those types of anxiety issues are among the strongest people I know.

Even if your first attempt wasn't successful, you at least stepped into the ring. That's a major step. It's a step that few people ever take. If you lost this round, no big deal. Just step back into the ring tomorrow. It may take a few weeks. But once you overcome that phobia, you'll be psychologically freer, and closer to a better life.

CHAPTER 5:

What Matters in Charity

Imagine two scenarios:

Scenario 1: A friend gives you a disgusting tasting pie that he baked. The pie took him hours to make; he made the dough from scratch, gave it time to rise, and a couple rounds in the freezer and fridge, rolled it out, poured in the filling that he mixed together himself, and baked it to a nice golden brown. But it just tastes terrible.

Scenario 2: A friend gives you a delicious pie that took him 2 minutes of easy work.

Which do you prefer?

Most people choose Scenario 2. They care more about the quality of what they receive than about how much pain the giver went through.

However, there is certainly a strain of thought that says charity is better when it hurts more. A person who gives his last dollar to charity is seen as more charitable than a rich person who gives a thousand dollars to charity. A person who donates $25 dollars to a charity is not as charitable as a person who donates $25 dollars AND walks 30 miles.

Charity has two functions. First, it benefits the recipient. Second, it makes the giver feel good about himself or herself. Usually, the more a person suffers in the act of giving charity, the better they feel about themselves.

But the reality is, the important part of charity is what the recipient gets, not how much the giver gets to suffer. How much the receiver's life improves matters way more than how much the giver gave up. The joy of the receiver matters. The discomfort of the giver does not.

From a purely economic sense, the best charity is the kind that benefits the recipient and doesn't give the giver any discomfort at all! That's what actually increases the joy in the world the most.

The first phase of Materialistic Minimalism involves donating the things that are holding you down. It involves donating the second-rate items so that you use your first-rate items.

If you have 50 scarves, you may end up donating most of them, to make sure you wear your best ones. If you have piles of costume jewelry, you may end up donating almost all of it, to make sure you start wearing real jewelry. If you have 90 pairs of shoes, you may end up donating all but the best few, in order to make sure you wear your best.

But where does all your second-rate stuff go? It

goes to people who benefit from it. People who can use it as their new first rate things. People who benefit greatly from that gently used (or never worn) jacket that you've had in your closet for years and years.

Over the past several years, I and others have donated huge amounts of our second-rate items. Unlike donating money, doing so doesn't really involve any kind of loss. The giver's life actually improves, since he now ends up using better things and improving his standard of living.

But the impact on the recipients has been just as large. For example, piles of costume jewelry went to kids with struggling single mothers. For some, it was the first necklace or bracelet they had ever had.

A lot of it was relatively fashionable. Your second-rate clothing and jewelry may well be outside the range of what another family can afford. Within days, the kids who were teased about their clothes were now the envy of their classmates because of their fashionable bracelets, necklaces, watches, and sunglasses. The items that had been doing nothing but taking up space were improving the lives of many children and families with limited economic means.

Much of the donated clothing went directly to parents or older kids. My old clothes helped dads who were working two or three jobs update their wardrobes. For the donors, the result was a higher standard of living. For the recipients, it was the same! No one suffered, and everyone was made better off.

Ownership, Selfishness, and Economics

What does it mean to own something? To own land? A jacket? A bracelet?

When you own something, it means you can use it, and other people cannot. You can wear this jacket, and other people cannot. Sure, you can let someone use it, but that's never the primary goal of ownership. Rarely do you buy something primarily to let strangers use it. If we all bought houses knowing that we would have to let other people use it, we certainly wouldn't pay quite so much for the ownership title.

There's nothing wrong with that. You want ready access to your coat so you can be warm and fashionable. You want ready access to your jewelry so you can look good when you want to. You want to have your home the way you like it, and only entertain when you choose.

But when many of us look deep into our closets, we find things that we aren't using. We don't even like them. We don't really want them. We're just keeping them to keep them.

When you do that, you're no longer saying, "I

own this so I can use it." Now you are saying, "I own this simply to prevent others from using it." Because that's all you're doing with it. You're saying, "I despise others so much, that I don't want anyone to have access to this shirt. I'd rather stuff it in my closet, making my own life worse, just to make sure no one else gets to use this shirt."

You're saying, "I hate this necklace, but I hate other people more. I'd rather make a mess of my dresser drawer than let someone else wear this necklace."

While each of us has the right to be petty and misanthropic, it's not a great idea It's not psychologically healthy. It makes your life worse, and it prevents you from making other people's lives better.

But when you take those items and say, "I don't really want this, and it can make someone else's life better," you are taking a step towards improving the lives of people around you, and your own life (not to mention that of anyone you share a closet with). When you choose charity over misanthropy, you win not just a more pleasant approach to life, but also a cleaner home, a shorter morning preparation time, and so much more. And you get to be happy knowing you improved the lives of people less fortunate than you just as much, if not more.

Now some part of you might think, "Wait, this isn't really improving someone else's life. It's just my second-rate stuff. This isn't real charity. If I am donating it specifically because it's not that great, then I'm basically saying the same thing about the recipients, right?" But that part of you is wrong.

If you play a musical instrument, imagine how overjoyed you would be if you got the backup guitar, flute, or saxophone of a famous musician as a gift. Imagine how excited you would be to receive Bill Gates' tenth favorite car.

For that matter, imagine how excited Bill Gates would be to receive the Queen of England's backup crown as a gift!

With a gift, the benefit to the recipient is what really matters. I know they say, "It's the thought that counts," but that's one of those sayings that is more polite than true. When you were a kid, your mom was probably happy when you made her a picture out of dried macaroni. But my guess: she'd be even happier if someone bought her a car.

With charity, it's not the thought that counts. It's the benefit that counts. And when you "selfishly" start to donate the things you don't really want, you'll also be benefiting many other individuals and families who do want those things.

That's not the empty feel-goodery that often passes as charity. That's real charity that makes a real difference in real people's lives.

CHAPTER 6:

The Next Exercise

If you completed the first exercise, it's time for the next one. If you didn't, just jump back to that chapter, and try that first exercise again.

In the first exercise, you donated a few things. That was a way to show yourself that you could. The compulsions associated with the Inner Hoarder are strong, but your will is strong too, and if a few days have passed, you've also seen the benefits.

At the very least, you have a bit more space in your closet or drawer. But it's also likely that you've started improving your standard of living. Maybe you're wearing slightly nicer clothes when you go to the grocery store. Maybe when you hang out with your friends you wear slightly nicer jewelry. You might have already noticed that you're getting treated subtly better wherever you go.

In the first exercise, you donated some of your tenth-rate stuff, so you would at least use your ninth-rate stuff. But now we need to gradually move you up. If you donate all your ninth-rate stuff, you'll at least use your eight-rate stuff.

If you continue that process, you'll gradually end up using exclusively your first-rate stuff. Without spending a cent, you will have increased your standard of living.

But you're probably not going to do that in a single day. Today, just try to fill a large bag with things to donate. If you don't have a large bag, use two grocery bags.

When you're deciding whether or not to keep a shirt, a pen, a scarf, a pair of sunglasses, or a random object, use this rule of thumb: If it's not a hell yes, it's a hell no.

CHAPTER 7:
The Three Checks

The number one reason we don't use our nice things is compulsion. We feel that we need to save them for special occasions, or for posterity. We feel like only arrogant, spoiled people use their nice things. Decent people politely never use them, so that their grandkids can sell them for $2 at an estate sale.

But there is another reason we don't use our nicer things. They are just too damned inconvenient.

Nice things are always breakable or high maintenance. Nice clothes often need to be dry cleaned, which is annoying, or hand washed, which is ludicrous. Nice objects break if you drop them, breathe near them, or look at them funny. Nice shoes get ruined easily. Nice pens require elaborate maintenance.

So, nice clothes end up sitting in the back of the closet. It's not that we don't like them or don't want to wear them. We just don't want to deal with their high maintenance annoyingness. Nice pens stay in a closet because we can't be bothered to deal with them. Nice jewelry stays in boxes, because it seems like it would be annoying to care for.

But what if it wasn't like that? What if your nicest things were also the most convenient? You'd probably use those things more willingly. If your nicest clothes were the most attractive and the least annoying, wouldn't that be a dream come true?

This chapter functions as both a buying guide and a keeping guide. It will help you decide what to donate and what to keep. But it will also help you decide what to buy (and what not to buy) in the future.

Materialistic Minimalism Makes You Richer

Before we get to the guidelines, it is important to realize that Materialistic Minimalists are functionally richer than mass consumers. Here's why:

The mass consumer buys 100 t-shirts. The Materialistic Minimalist buys 10. That means that the Materialistic Minimalist can spend a lot more per shirt. Even if he spends 9 times as much per shirt, the Materialistic Minimalist spends less in total!

That also means that Materialistic Minimalists can be a lot more picky. After all, their budget per item is ten times as high as the budget of a mass consumer. The mass consumer must buy a lot of junk, and that's expensive. The Materialistic Minimalist buys very few items, and each one is excellent.

The mass consumer may buy 30 scarves for $10 each. The Materialistic Minimalist buys one scarf for $100. Given that both people only have one neck each, the Materialistic Minimalist ends up looking and feeling a lot better, and saves $200.

As a Materialistic Minimalist, you can afford to be a lot more picky than a mass consumer. You are richer, since you buy far fewer things, so you can spend extra to get higher quality items.

So now let's talk about how to be picky.

When you are deciding whether or not to buy something, it must meet three criteria. We call them "The Three Checks." They are: The Engineering Check, The Aesthetic Check, and the Materials Check. Making sure every single thing you buy, and every single thing you keep, passes these three checks will result in a quantum improvement in your standard of living.

The First Check: The Engineering Check

The first, and most important check is the Engineering Check. In this check, you make sure that whatever you plan to buy (or keep) is sturdy, convenient, and easy to care for.

Technically, it is the easiest check. Emotionally, it is the hardest.

Let's talk about the technical aspects first.

With clothing, it means make sure whatever you

buy is machine washable and machine dryable.

This is hard, because many very attractive items of clothing are dry clean only. But the fact is: if you buy that fancy, dry clean only item, it will sit in your closet. You'll wear it a couple times, and then hide it away rather than take it to the dry cleaner.

Sometimes, we imagine a glamorously disciplined life, in which we will be organized, disciplined, and get dry cleaning done every day. If you have already been doing that for years, great. If you "plan" to do it in the future but haven't done it yet: you're most likely dreaming. Most people who buy something expensive or inconvenient in the hope that doing so will change their habits do not get the results they hope for. The millions of treadmills rotting away in basements across the country helps illustrate that.

"Dry Clean Only" is really just Latin for "Worn Twice Only."

The same applies to clothes that need to be hand washed. When you're tired, you will always prefer whatever is most convenient. When you are not tired, you'll still prefer whatever is most convenient. On every day of the week, at every time of the day, you will prefer what is most convenient. So, make sure your best clothes are the most convenient.

The good news is, many nice clothes can be machine washed! Most modal, cotton, silk, and silk blends can be machine washed. These materials are also pretty durable. Even some wool blends are washable, although most are not.

Sometimes clothes made out of these materials are slightly more expensive. But remember, as a Materialistic Minimalist, you can spend much more per item, since you will be buying fewer items.

In addition, while a silk item of clothing that can be washed may cost more than a synthetic rayon one that must be dry cleaned, you will end up using it more. That means you will pay much less per use. A $20 shirt you wear one time costs $20 per use. A $50 shirt you wear 100 times costs 50 cents per use. It's the more intelligent purchase.

Remember: convenient doesn't mean low quality or ugly. Silk is convenient, but no one considers it junky. The same is true of cotton and modal.

What about jewelry? The same rules apply. Only buy jewelry that passes the engineering check.

Don't worry – plenty of nice jewelry passes the engineering check. Platinum is called the indestructible metal of kings for a reason. Diamonds are the strongest things on earth. Rubies and sapphires are the second strongest. Jewelry made of platinum and diamonds usually passes the engineering check. No one considers it junky.

But not all jewelry passes the engineering check! Pearls do not. When you wear pearls, you have to worry about damaging them, so you end up not wearing them.

Emeralds are on the border. They are hard, but a little more brittle than sapphires. Don't worry: jade and green diamonds both pass the engineering check, and are just as green as emeralds. So does alexandrite, which is a gem that appears green in natural light and red in artificial light. There is no shortage of limitlessly exquisite jewelry that passes the engineering check.

The Buddy System

Many people find it helpful to use a buddy system for the engineering check.

According to the philosopher Robert Pirsig (author of *Zen and the Art of Motorcycle Maintenance*), most people have either a classical or romantic way of seeing the world. Classical people are concerned with underlying forms of things. They care about functionality more than aesthetics. Most engineers have a classical mindset.

Those with romantic mindsets, on the other side, are more attuned to the surface aesthetics of things. They are more affected by appearance than by underlying functionality. Most art history majors have a romantic mindset.

When practicing Materialistic Minimalism, it's great to use a buddy system. If you have a classical mindset, find someone with a romantic mindset to be your buddy, and vice versa. Then, when considering whether to buy something, have your buddy check it as well.

Your buddy doesn't have to be your spouse or significant other, and it doesn't have to be someone of the opposite sex. It just has to be someone who can see the important facts about clothing that you don't see.

Even I have a Materialistic Minimalist buddy! I provide the classic insights, and she provides the romantic insights.

For me, the classical part is easy. When my romantic buddy asks about an item of clothing she really likes, I just glance at the label. If I see dry clean only, or hand wash only, or lay flat to dry, or anything like that, I veto it.

But the aesthetic part is hard for me. We'll talk about that in the next section, but as the name suggests, it's checking to make sure something looks good. The good news: the aesthetics part is really easy for my Materialistic Minimalist buddy!

The buddy system rules are pretty straightforward: either buddy can veto anything. It takes unanimous agreement to buy something.

Obviously, that means you will buy fewer things, but each thing will be both attractive and convenient.

Exceptions

There are some notable exceptions to the Engineering Check, although not many. These exceptions are based on what currently exists in the world.

For example, a few years ago, there were no washable and presentable business suits. So, at that time, you had to buy dry clean only business suits.

But that's already changed. The company Ministry of Supply, created by an MIT graduate, makes suits that are washable and resilient. In fact, you can even bike in them.

If those suits aren't at all your style, then you'll probably have to settle for a suit that has to be dry cleaned. But the number of convenient options is increasing every year.

The rule for exceptions: if there is literally no convenient option available on earth, and for some reason you absolutely need that item, get what is least inconvenient.

This will not apply to a significant percent of the

things you buy, or the things you decide not to donate. 90 percent or more of your clothes will be able to pass the engineering check. 100% of your jewelry will also pass it.

Pro tips: Specialization vs. Versatility

It can be hard to find clothes that pass the engineering check. The good news is that more and more companies are designing clothes that are attractive enough to wear around, and durable enough to wear while working out! In other words, they don't just pass the engineering check. They exceed it!

Lululemon Athletica has quite a few clothes that meet this high standard. So do many of their competitors. Hanro is another great company.

These companies create clothes that are a bit more expensive. But first, remember that since Materialistic Minimalists buy fewer things, they can spend more per item. And second, consider that these clothes can be used for multiple purposes. A single shirt can be a going out shirt and a working out shirt. It could even potentially work with a blazer for casual Friday at work. This will help you further reduce the number of clothes you have, decreasing clutter, increasing space, and improving your standard of living.

When you can use the same shirt for multiple purposes, the cost per use decreases. You may end up using the shirt 1000 times, instead of 3 times. Even though the shirt costs more, because you use it more often, it costs much less per use.

Today, when I buy an item of clothing, I try to find something that I can use for working out and going out. Most items of clothing cannot pass that high standard. But the ones that do are exceptional, and wearing them enhances my daily life, and ensures that I am ready for any situation at any time.

Versatility has a huge adaptability advantage. Versatile clothes help you quickly adjust to unexpected circumstances. If you were planning to go to a casual bar, but end up going to a fancy reception instead, it's ideal to have versatile clothing that will look good in both scenarios.

Versatile clothing also takes up much less space. Each versatile item of clothing replaces several non-versatile items. That's great for clearing out your closet.

Incidentally, it's also great for travel! In the past, when most of my clothing was specialized, packing was a chore. I never knew what situations I would get into in the other country, so I had to prepare for all kinds of possibilities. My suitcase would be huge and heavy. Despite that, I would always run out of the clothes I actually needed in the destination country. I invariably had enough clothing for one day of cold weather, but not two days. Or for two days of fancy restaurants, but not three.

Today, I don't need a suitcase. If I am bringing a suit, I carry a light garment bag. If not, a simple back-pack gets the job done. I always have the clothes I need, since each item of clothing can be used in a variety of situations.

Consider, for example, the inevitably variable weather you can experience on any vacation. If you're traveling in the late Fall or Winter, you could get snow or cold winds. Or, it could end up being pretty balmy. You could pack shorts, jeans, long underwear, light socks, heavy socks, several shirt layers, and a few jackets, just in case, not to mention your workout clothes. Or you could have a few pairs of socks that work in all weather (hiking socks are great for this), workout pants that double as long underwear and casual going around pants if the weather gets warmer, and a jacket that can accommodate very cold and only slightly chilly temperatures.

In short, you can cut your total packing by about two-thirds when things serve multiple purposes.

But, what about specialization? Sometimes apparel dedicated to a specific task is better than versatile attire. This is not often true; most of my current clothing is better in every possible situation than my old, specialized clothing was in each specialized situation. (Versatility, of course, demands a much higher level of thought in the creation process, and therefore leads to a higher quality product overall.)

However, sometimes specialization is actually the way to go. For example, wedding dresses and tuxedos don't really need to be versatile. Even if you theoretically could create a wedding dress that could also be used for working out, wearing such a thing to the gym would make you look like a lunatic.

In those situations, renting is often better than buying. It rarely makes sense to actually purchase something you intend to use only once. You can spend the same amount of money and rent a dress twice as nice.

If you do decide to buy a dress, donate or sell it the day after the wedding. For the love of all that is holy don't save it for your daughter's or granddaughter's wedding. No dress on earth is worth saving, and not wearing, as 30 years, let alone 50 years, of fashion go by. Even if you think your daughter will use it in 30 years, you should still donate it and help her select the dress of her own dreams. And, of course, some people never have daughters. When you take all the factors into account, saving the dress becomes really silly.

On the other hand, if you plan to get remarried once a week, you should buy and keep the dress.

The Second Check: The Aesthetics Check

If you have a classical mindset, you probably enjoyed reading the last section. You may have thought about a friend, significant other, parent, child, or spouse who you couldn't wait to show that chapter to. You may have thought, "Finally, someone understands practicality. Someone sees that it's silly to buy high-maintenance things and never use them. Someone gets that things should actually be functional, not just pretty."

All of that is true. But now it's your turn.

The second check is the Aesthetics Check. That means in order to buy or keep something, it must look good.

Yes, even electronics and tools. And obviously all clothes, jewelry, shoes, etc.

If you have a classical mindset, you really, absolutely must get a Materialistic Minimalist buddy with a romantic mindset! Have that person review every purchase.

You're probably wondering: who on earth cares if a tool looks good? Who cares if electronic equipment looks good. What difference could it possibly make?

First, it's important to realize that looking good doesn't mean covered with a flower pattern or painted with rainbows. A good aesthetic appearance often comes from a balanced proportionality which indicates intelligent craftsmanship.

Second, centuries ago, master sword makers would put serious effort into the aesthetics of the weapons they constructed. It was their way of letting the buyer know that they were buying a finished piece, not a half-done experiment.

When a tool or electronic item has an aesthetically intelligent appearance, it conveys that the maker has put a little extra thought into his work. Chances are, the maker also put effort into getting the other details right. For him, this item is a masterpiece, not some barely considered side project.

The things that I have bought that passed both the engineering and aesthetic checks have often surprised me with the little, unexpected details they got right. Often, I didn't notice until I had already been using the item for a few days, but it was always great to be pleasantly surprised.

On the other hand, items that seemed perfectly functional but had a poor aesthetic appearance often later annoyed me because of their unexpected short-comings.

While aesthetics might not matter directly, they can be a signal that the item has been considered carefully by the maker. It lets you know that the maker took pride in his work, and probably got the details right.

Great armorers, silversmiths, blacksmiths, cobblers, and tailors of the past, cared deeply about their work. They took pains to get every detail right – including the aesthetics.

Today, many great manufacturers care just as deeply about their work. While many companies are happy to produce indifferent junk, there are still those who really care about their work. Buy their products, and you won't regret it.

A popular saying in India is, "He who buys something expensive cries once. He who buys something cheap cries again and again." Cry once, and then enjoy the high-quality item for a lifetime.

"Exclusive", Trendy Fashion Almost Never Passes the 3 Checks

With clothes, expensive doesn't automatically mean good. It almost never means convenient. To be honest, it often doesn't even mean aesthetically attractive.

Most "high end" clothes do not pass the three

checks. Just because a shirt costs $2000, doesn't mean it's worth buying.

Instead of letting fashion become an expensive hobby, go past that. Look for clothes that make you look your best. Instead of trying to follow trends, set yourself above transient foolishness. Cultivate your own, defined, iconic look. Build your own brand and recognizable appearance. Be a fashion leader, not a desperate follower.

Use the Three Checks to make sure you are getting excellent clothes that enhance your life. Your goal is not to make fashion designers rich; it's to make yourself look good.

The Third Check: The Materials Check

The thing I love most about Materialistic Minimalism is that it gives you access to much better things. Instead of having 900 mediocre things, you have 9 incredible things.

The problem is, it's not actually that simple to find high quality things!

Some people try to take the easy way out, and just buy more expensive things. That doesn't really work. Many "elite" brands just sell mediocre things at huge markups.

Other people rely on online reviews. That can

help a little, but they are much less reliable than you might think. I've seen mediocre and exceptional items have literally the same star ratings on Amazon. In fact, sometimes mediocre things have higher star ratings! People generally incorporate price into their rating, and lower priced things get more stars. Unfortunately, lower priced things are often just worse.

Other people rely on recommendations from friends, but most of our friends are mass consumers, not Materialistic Minimalists. They just don't hold material items to a high enough standard.

I've made all of these mistakes. I've tried buying the most expensive things. I've tried relying on reviews. I've tried recommendations from friends. None of that worked. (The obvious exception is friends who are themselves Materialistic Minimalists and can therefore give great advice!)

I developed The Three Checks as a way to ensure I was only buying and keeping things of the highest quality. Some things that pass the three checks are expensive. Interestingly, others are not.

The final check is the Materials Check. It's technically a little harder than the engineering check, but psychologically easier.

The rationale is a little less transparent. The Engineering Check is necessary for obvious reasons: when an object is inconvenient you won't use it.

Buying clothing that fails the engineering check is equivalent to setting money on fire and then putting trash into your closet.

But the Materials Check serves a different purpose: it helps to ensure that you are buying high quality items, rather than mediocre junk.

Here's how it works: Whenever you buy an item, make sure that it is constructed of a high-quality material, rather than an inferior substitute.

For example, if you see a t-shirt that says, "As soft as cotton, but half the price!" don't buy it. Whenever something is "As great as something else, but...", it is just an inferior substitute.

In clothing, that often means buying natural materials like cotton, modal, bamboo, or silk. But it's not always that simple. For example, buying a jacket made out of cotton wouldn't make much sense. Materials like Gore-Tex, while synthetic, are often the best relevant material available.

With jewelry, it's easier: don't buy costume jewelry. No matter how pretty a piece of glass or plastic jewelry is, it's not worth it. Instead, buy jewelry made of something exceptional.

That will mean that you may end up with a much smaller amount of jewelry. That's an improvement. Instead of a lot of mediocre things, you'll have a small number of exceptional things. Each day, you'll not only look better, but also connect yourself with something of real thought and value.

Furniture made of real hardwoods, carbon fiber, or other superior materials will surpass furniture made from cheap particle board. A fountain pen made of gold, jade, exotic wood, or other rare materials will often be superior to one made of plastic.

It should be noted that the materials check does not always mean that you should buy things made of the most expensive material. There are often other considerations. For example, even a billionaire may prefer a watch made of titanium rather than platinum. Although platinum is considered the more elite material, titanium is much lighter. Many find a heavy watch to be uncomfortable. Some of the nicest fountain pens are made of titanium as well, instead of gold. But in those cases, there will be other strong signals that indicate high quality in an item.

The majority of the time, you can seek the highest quality materials as your primary indicator of excellence in construction. No one is going to make a rickety table out of granite. No one will make a crappy, breakable pen out of solid gold. It's just too much trouble to use high quality materials, so when makers use such materials, you can reasonably assume they put some thought into their designs.

Implications of the Three Checks

For me, some parts of Materialistic Minimalism were easy. Donating bags of old t-shirts gave me a huge sense of relief.

But other parts were hard. I had a large collection of leather jackets. When it came down to it, not a single one could pass the Engineering Check.

While they were waterproofed, none were great in the rain. I still had to worry about water damage to the jacket, and in an unexpected downpour they certainly did not keep me dry.

Cleaning any of them would have been a huge, annoying production. Instead of throwing them into the washing machine, or even taking them to a dry cleaner, I would have had to take them to a leather cleaning specialist.

In fairness, most didn't really pass the aesthetic check either. I had bought many of them on my own, without a Materialistic Minimalist buddy to perform the aesthetic check.

After much searching, I ended up replacing a closet full of leather jackets with my one, Arcteryx Fission SL jacket. This particular jacket is made of Gore-Tex, so it is waterproof. Unlike the leather jackets, it can be easily washed. It is also a lot warmer than even my shearling coat.

I gave the nicer of my leather jackets to friends, family members, and others. I donated many of the average ones.

For me, there have been many benefits. First, I have a lot more closet space. Second, I'm pretty much always ready for any situation. When it unexpectedly rains, I just put up the hood. If it's unusually cold, I'm ready. If it's warmer than expected, I can just open the side vents of the jacket. If I get splashed with mud or hit with bird droppings, I just throw the jacket into the washing machine.

Moving from a closet full of jackets to one highly versatile jacket, while initially difficult, has been one of the biggest improvements in my life.

I did the same with shoes. I have a lot fewer shoes than I used to. It just makes my life better, since I only wear the ones that are the most versatile and attractive, and of course the most comfortable.

Going through the things you have, and applying the three checks, can be kind of fun. It's especially great when you have too much of a particular item, and don't know what to do.

I have had quite a few friends that had too many scarves. Those who believe in treating all clothes equally would end up wearing a different scarf each day of the month. They only got to wear their best scarf once a month, and had to deal with lower quality, less comfortable, or less attractive scarves the rest of the time.

Others ended up just wearing the same two or three scarves repeatedly. But of course, these weren't usually their best scarves, just some arbitrarily chosen few. Whatever scarf was the most recent was the most accessible, so it got worn more often.

This is one of those problems that tends to grow all by itself. When people see you have a lot of scarves, guess what they all try to get you for your birthday. For other holidays. Just because they were thinking of you.

Through gifts, the number of scarves multiplied like bacteria. And trying to decide which ones to keep through traditional methods became impossible. Do I keep the one from my best friend, my significant other, or my roommate? This one reminds me of Italy, but this one is made of Italian silk. What do I do?

In a panic, some people would try to donate one or two scarves, and then give up. Others would just look at the sea of scarves and give up preemptively.

But with the three checks, things became much, much easier. Scarves made of acrylic or synthetic rayon were automatically donated. That cleared up about half. Those that were in any way uncomfortable were donated. So were the ones that were of a non-ideal color.

Within minutes, we were able to effectively reduce the number of scarves to just the first and second rate scarves.

We'll talk about how to narrow things down further soon, but now it's time for the next exercise.

CHAPTER 8:
Exercise 3: Apply the Three Checks

Before you apply the Engineering Check, the Aesthetics Check, and the Materials Check to new purchases, apply them to things you already own. Using these checks takes some practice, and you don't want to buy something that you have to donate a month later when you better understand the checks. So, before you spend any money on new things, see if you can apply these principles to what you already have.

At this point, you can be a bit bolder. Pick something that you have a lot of: T-shirts, scarves, jackets, pants. Apply the Three Checks in order to whittle down the number. You might be able to get rid of 80 percent of that group!

You'll be left with the best; you will wear or use only your best. The best shirts, the best scarves, the best earrings, you name it.

If you're sorting through earrings, you could end up with a shopping bag full of costume jewelry that was eliminated by the Materials Check. Donate it, and help a child with no jewelry at all feel special.

If you're donating t-shirts, you might have two or three trash bags full, and a much more manageable closet. When you donate it, someone with less money will have access to a whole new wardrobe.

If you're getting rid of scarves, you'll be wearing much better, more comfortable, more attractive scarves. The rest will find new homes, and bring joy to those who could not have afforded them before.

During the next few days and weeks, keep on applying the Three Checks to different items. One after another, each of those areas will improve. It will be like having a Midas touch, but instead of all your items turning indiscriminately to gold, they will become the best version of that thing.

When you reach for a scarf, you'll be reaching for your best scarf. When you put on a shirt, you'll be putting on your best one. When you put on a bracelet, you'll be putting on something exceptional. When you write, you'll be using a nice pen, like a senator, instead of a disposable pen, like a sixth grader.

Replacement

As you go through your things, many of them will fail one or more of the three checks. At that point, you should donate it. But, sometimes the thing that fails will be your only remaining plain white shirt, or your only remaining pair of jeans. You won't want to throw those things out because they are necessary, staple pieces of a wardrobe.

That's fine. Then your primary goal should become finding an excellent replacement for that item. When you do, donate the thing that didn't meet the three checks, and use only your new, higher quality shirt or pair of pants.

Replacement will be a major focus in the beginning. It will help ensure you have all the necessary wardrobe items, and ease you into the process of donating most of what you currently own.

Replacement, though, should not be used for ridiculous items. If you have a dry-clean only, sequined, bright purple blouse and matching shoes, you should not focus on replacing those with a shirt and shoes that happen to meet the 3 Checks. You should still focus on building a simplified, calming overall wardrobe, which we will discuss more later on.

Other Examples of Using the 3 Checks

We've talked about using the 3 Checks for clothes and jewelry. But they also apply in other surprising areas.

Glassware

Many of us have a set of nice glassware, and junky daily use glasses. Nice wine glasses are just too annoying to use daily. They need to be hand washed, break easily, and are a general nuisance. We save them for "special occasions" because they are inconvenient.

But many companies have started making nice glassware that is also resilient. For example, Schott Zweisel makes glassware out of a titanium crystal. This makes their glassware stronger, and capable of being machine washed. Instead of having nice glasses and daily use glasses, you can make your nice glasses your daily use glasses!

Furniture

So many people buy furniture that passes the Aesthetic Check, but comes nowhere close to passing the other two. Buying a couch in a fabric that requires an elaborate cleaning process will make your life less pleasant. A couch made out of white fabric has essentially the same effect.

A couch made of leather or a high-quality synthetic will make your life much easier. If you really love fabric, consider one with easily replaceable cushions.

The biggest mistake people make in buying furniture is disregarding the Engineering Check. This usually ends with a half broken, sagging couch that gets moved down to your basement. It's out of sight, out of mind, but still taking up space.

Furniture can, however, meet all three checks, and

when it does, it adds greatly to your own enjoyment of your home, the happiness of guests when you have them over, and the overall functionality and ease of your space.

CHAPTER 9:

Minimalism vs. Hoarding: The Value of Space and Time

Every lifestyle has advantages and disadvantages. There are some benefits to living in the city and some to living in the mountains.

Similarly, there are advantages to Materialistic Minimalism, just as there are advantages to hoarding.

I've gotten to see both sides. I grew up with a hoarding father. I've personally engaged in mid-level hoarding. And I've done Materialistic Minimalism. There are advantages and drawbacks.

In my early childhood, my dad had one room in our three bedroom apartment dedicated to junk. Later, when we moved into a house, the two car garage was filled from floor to ceiling with all kinds of everything.

My parents have never had the luxury of parking a car in their two car garage. It's jammed from floor to ceiling with tools, spare parts, and god knows what else.

Today, I occasionally use my dad's garage as a kind of "scared straight" program to encourage people to adopt Materialistic Minimalism.

But the reality is, there were some advantages to that garage full of everything in the universe.

If I needed something for a science fair project, there was probably something usable in the garage. If I lost a pen cap, there was a spare one somewhere in the garage. If I wanted to polish a stone, there was probably something in that packed garage.

But there were also major inconveniences. It would often take my dad and I (mostly my dad) hours to find a minor item. It might actually take us two or three hours to find a particular screw or nail. In that amount of time, we could easily have just gone to the hardware store and gotten whatever we needed. While my dad was not a millionaire, he certainly made more than 3 cents an hour. Spending 3 hours looking for a 9-cent item just didn't make sense.

And then of course, the things we could find were usually not an exact match. A spare pen cap would more or less fit the pen that needed it, but it would be a constant annoyance, since it didn't fit right. It wouldn't go on all the way, or be just loose enough to be about to fall off. The screws might be too big or too small, furniture varnish was probably banned several years prior, and the huge sheets of plastic and rubber were just enormous, inexplicable, and permanently useless.

Hours were spent searching to get a not-right item, sorting through countless things no one could ever use. A ten-minute trip to a drug store and a $2 expenditure would have gotten a perfect match with no hassle.

The Value of Time

Time is a valuable quantity. You know the market value of your time: it's your hourly wage, or the hourly wage of a job you could reasonably get.

That hourly wage applies to all of your time, not just the time you spend working, because you could theoretically work more hours, or get a second job with similar pay.

None of your time is worthless. All of it is valuable.

When comparing lifestyles, consider that value carefully. If you are spending three hours searching for a $3 thing, and you make more than $1 per hour, you are making a bad decision.

Even if you are a stay at home mom or dad, your time is not worthless. If you want a number, compare it to what a babysitter who cared as much about your kids as you do would charge, or to how much you would make at another job you would be likely to get. That is the hourly value of your time.

If you have so many things that it takes you hours to find things, you are making bad economic decisions. You are spending your hourly wage times the number of hours spent searching for things. Are the things you are looking for actually that valuable? Is that roll of tape really worth $70?

What if you donated everything you "might one day need"? How much time would you save, compared to how much money you would need to spend re-buying the thing?

In my own situation, I have donated several pickup truckloads of things. Every so often, I end up needing one of those things. It doesn't happen very often, but it does happen. In those cases, I have to buy a new item.

During the last year, because of this, I have spent maybe an extra $30. But I have also saved many hours that I might have otherwise spent searching. Economically, even if you have to occasionally re-buy something, you will come out way ahead. You'll save the most precious resource of all: time.

The Value of Space

It's obvious that space has market value. You pay more rent or a higher mortgage for a larger home. You pay more for larger retail space. Businesses pay for warehouse space or shelf space in stores. You can pay for storage space.

You can even rent out part of your own house, if you want to. You can rent out extra rooms, or even rent out storage space. If you want to place a price tag on your space, just ask how much you would charge a stranger if they wanted to store something on your shelf, or in your garage. Maybe it would be $20 a month. Maybe more. It probably isn't $0 a month.

That's one way to approximate the market value of that space.

Another way: just measure how much you are paying for that space. If you have a 1500 square foot house, and you are using 500 square feet for storage, then you are paying one third of your mortgage or rent for storage.

But is whatever you are storing really worth that much? Are you actually storing tens of thousands of dollars' worth of valuable material in that space? Or is it just $20 worth of junk?

Even more than market value, space actually has an intrinsic value. I cannot begin to describe the calm of looking at a mostly empty closet or cupboard.

When you look at jammed clutter, it creates stress and tension. When you look at minimalism, it creates tranquility.

Taoist philosophers, productivity experts, and famous architects all know that a minimalistic environment, free of clutter, improves your life. It brings peacefulness, assuages frustrations, and increases focus and productivity. When you eliminate clutter, you prepare yourself to be more effective in other areas of your life.

CHAPTER 10:

Strategically Refine Your Wardrobe for Stronger First Impressions

One of my favorite writers goes by the pseud-onym, The Watch Snob. He writes about fancy swiss watches, and often answers readers' questions with humorous arrogance.

One reader was considering a very expensive Patek Philippe watch (the price was in the neighborhood of $100,000). The reader's concern was that the strap and the dial of the watch were blue. This is often done with platinum watches, since doing so brings out the natural bluish tint in the platinum metal.

Unfortunately for the reader, his attire, particu-larly his belt and shoes, were black. A blue watch would be a poor match.

The Watch Snob's solution was to get the watch, and then get new shoes and a new belt. Get rid of everything that was black, and embrace the color blue. After all, if you can afford such an expensive watch, you can certainly afford a new pair of dress shoes.

For most of us, an imagined need for varied dress ends up limiting the quality of what we can afford. The aforementioned watch buyer could clearly afford an expensive, platinum, Patek Philippe watch. But it's unlikely that he could have afforded ten in different colors.

He could certainly have afforded several comparatively mediocre watches in a variety of colors. But in going that route, he would have separated himself from something truly exceptional. Instead of an extraordinary watch, he would have had several lesser watches.

The variety of lower quality watches has one major advantage: it allows him to vary the color palette of his attire. But the huge drawback is that variety does not translate into excellence. Sure, he can look different on different days, but that's not the same as looking better.

Suppose he had chosen to buy 7 mediocre watches instead of the one, great watch (one for every day of the week). Suppose it's Wednesday, after work, and a friend introduces him to someone of influence. The aforementioned buyer is wearing a Wednesday watch – nothing special. But he wishes he was wearing something exceptional for this meeting. He's wearing clothes that match his Wednesday watch. The clothes are fine, but not exceptional. He has to come up with several different looks, so none of them can get his full attention, nor the full force of his monetary investment.

The same principle holds true if that friend introduces him to an attractive person he may be romantically interested in. Or to the CEO of the company. Or to an investor. Or to someone in the media.

Like you, that watch buyer only gets one chance to make a first impression.

Everyone has colors that look good on them. Of those colors that look good, some look better. Some look the best.

The same is true with metal jewelry. Some people look better with gold; others look better with silver or platinum.

The same is true with gemstones. There is some stone that looks the best on you.

Everyone has to make a choice between variety and excellence. You can choose to have 200 pairs of earrings that cost $10 each, or one pair of earrings that costs a few thousand.

If you are extremely wealthy, the same rules apply. Just move the decimal point a bit. There are earrings that cost ten or one hundred times as much, and are correspondingly better. Instead of getting twenty different sets of ruby earrings, why not consider an exceptional pair of red diamond earrings?

We know that a thousand fools don't make a wise man. Similarly, a thousand mediocre earrings don't make an exceptional pair of earrings. A thousand mediocre rings don't make an exceptional ring. A thousand mediocre watches don't make an exceptional watch.

Clothes need to be washed, so it's not practical to have just one of each item of clothing. But jewelry does not. You can wear the same piece of exceptional jewelry every day, instead of alternating junk.

First Impressions Matter; 101st Impressions Do Not

We often say to ourselves, "When I'm invited to the ambassador's home, then I'll wear my nice jewelry." Or, "When I get invited to some elite soiree, then we will break out that beautiful dress."

The problem: if you look your second (or tenth) best all the time, you are less likely to have those opportunities in the first place!

Even fairy tales get this. Cinderella had her wardrobe transformed *before* she met the Prince, not after. The first time the Prince laid eyes on her, he fell in love.

Later, when he saw her in her usual state, dirty and cleaning fireplaces, it didn't make much of a difference. The first impression had already been made.

We often say to ourselves, "If I wear similar clothes all the time, then my friends and coworkers will always see me look about the same. I need to wear a variety so that they see me differently."

But the fact is: it doesn't matter what your friends, family, or coworkers see.

You can choose your friends, but you can't choose your family. You're stuck with your family, but your family is also stuck with you. No matter what you choose to wear, you're still their family.

Your friends can theoretically stop being friends with you. But I have yet to hear of a friendship ending, or even being slightly strained, because one friend wore the same blue diamond earrings daily.

Your coworkers' opinions matter less than those of your friends. Your coworkers are at your level; they have no major ability to influence your opportunities. They can't promote you. And generally, they won't really notice your wardrobe much, unless you wear ridiculous clown colors to work every day (in which case you'll be mocked) or you wear something exceedingly fancy (in which case you'll be envied).

Your coworkers see you daily, but if you work for a large company, your CEO may see you only once a year. The first impression you make on your CEO will make a much larger difference than the 101st impression you make on the person in the adjacent cubicle.

Opportunities are random, unpredictable, and unexpected. But if you wear your best jewelry and ideal color palette every day, you will always be ready to make something of those opportunities.

Clothes for Special Occasions

Sometimes, as we've seen, we get clothes, or save clothes, based on unlikely fantasies. We say, "If I have this tuxedo, I'm going to get invited to the White House every week," or "If I have this dress, I'll end up going to more events at the Embassy of Monaco." Those expensive items sit, unused, in the closet.

But sometimes we save clothing for events that are more likely. Constantly afraid that one day we'll get invited to a last minute, themed dance party, or Halloween party, we save every ridiculous article of clothing we never wear.

This goes even farther. We might, one day, get invited to a square dance, so we should save these 18 flannel shirts, just to have choices. We might, one day, get invited to a Simpsons themed party, so we must keep this blue hairspray that expired 2 years ago. We may, next year, want to be a vampire for Halloween, so we have to store several wigs, capes, sets of fangs, and boxes of face paint forever.

Very quickly, this thought process gets out of control. While you may get invited to a costumed party, you will likely have more than 6 minutes' notice. You can easily go to a goodwill and buy what you need then, or order things on Amazon and get them in two days.

While you may, in fact, want to be a vampire next year for Halloween, you'll likely forget you have piles of Halloween costume items in storage, or you'll remember but the things will be dusty and will smell bad, or, even worse, rats will have moved into your Halloween storage box. No matter how you look at it, it's easier to just buy a new $20-$40 costume each year, be something new and fresh, and then donate the costume and never have to store anything at all.

When I dress up for Halloween, I donate the costume the day after. If the next year I don't really want to pay the cost of a new costume, then I understand dressing up is not that important to me. If I am unwilling to pay the cost of a dinner in order to dress up, then I don't dress up. But remember, you pay far more than the cost of a dinner to store piles of dress up clothes every year, taking up space in your apartment or house that costs money largely based on its square footage. Storage is really expensive, really stressful, and really not worth it.

Exercise 4: Build Your Color Palette

Jewelry costs more than clothes (unless you are buying plastic garbage jewelry). So, we begin with jewelry. First, determine if you look better with gold or silver/platinum. Then decide what precious stones make you look the best.

If you have not already done so, donate the rest of your costume jewelry. You're an adult. There is no reason for you to wear plastic or semi-precious jewelry any more.

Once you have determined the right jewelry color (and gotten rid of everything else), then determine what color palette looks the best on you. That palette should be between two and five colors (including black and white), and should also match the jewelry. If that doesn't work, you may need to reconsider the primary stone of the jewelry, but realistically it should work fine.

Many men take the simple solution and make their wardrobes entirely black and white. It's simple and versatile.

Some women find that this works just as well for them. A primarily black wardrobe combined with a jewelry accent can look quite striking.

Others find that all black doesn't really work for them. That's no big deal. All black doesn't work for Facebook, Coca Cola, or many other brands that spend millions refining their color palettes. Just like them, you can find a color palette that works well for you.

But don't fall into the false dichotomy that suggests the choices are either all black or every carnival color under the sun. That is preposterous. Your color palette may be primarily green and white. Sky blue and brown may work for you. There are limitless possibilities, but one that will be the best for you. Within that palette, you may have a few different outfits.

This is a good time to get advice from your Materialistic Minimalist buddy, or even from a professional wardrobe consultant. Explain to the professional that your goal is to limit your total number of clothes and to use a simple color palette that helps you make the best possible first impression. He or she will know what to do.

In fact, there are many cheap, online services that help you do just that! Many companies and blogs will help you create a "capsule wardrobe" by narrowing down your items to a small number of things that can be used together cleverly to create the illusion of varied outfits. Countless people have done this to combat shopping addictions, insane wardrobes, chaotic closets, and much more. Of the reviews I've seen, the vast majority were exceedingly pleased.

Once you limit your color palette to what actually makes you look your best, you open the door to truly exceptional things. You can stop worrying about trying to fit unflattering colors into your wardrobe. You never have to worry about wearing anything unflattering at all. You can achieve a peacefulness that comes with an organized closet and a simple selection of attractive, comfortable clothes every morning.

And you will likely save a lot of money. Even if you spend ten times more than a mass consumer, that mass consumer is often buying 300-500 items of clothing (some buy far more than that). With small, carefully crafted color palettes and an intentionally curated wardrobe, you will always look better, and will have higher quality purchases to be proud of.

What Do You Do With Extra Jewelry?

Suppose that you have a platinum and ruby ring that makes you look your best. What do you do with your other rings?

If they are costume jewelry, donate them or give them away.

If they are gold, keep them or sell them.

If they are made of $10 of silver, give them as gifts. While silver is technically "real", it's nowhere near as expensive as gold.

Just keep them away from yourself. If they are there, you'll be tempted to wear them. And there is no advantage to wearing your second-best ring on the day you happen to run into your CEO, your senator, or your potential soulmate.

CHAPTER 11:
Lessons from the Military

Many people find men in uniform to be attractive. But it's not just any uniform. With respect to our brothers in the foodservice industry, fast food uniforms are not particularly fetishized.

It's military uniforms that really excite. Military uniforms look good. Part of that is through the association with physical strength, and the corresponding masculine connotations. But part of that is that military uniforms just look good. They are just aesthetically appealing.

This is surprising, since the Federal Government can never seem to get anything right. Whether they are bungling education or just generally being inefficient and wasteful, we tend not to consider the Federal Government to be paragons of effectiveness.

But against all probability, the military found people who are good at fashion, so good at fashion that people literally fetishize their fashion.

I think the reason is pretty simple. They just don't make that many different uniforms. Everyone at a similar level in the Navy, for example, wears the same dress uniform. Those at a higher level wear very similar dress uniforms, with small adjustments.

Instead of trying to create fifty different uniforms, they put all their effort into a single dress uniform, and a single combat uniform. And when they do that, they end up getting it right.

If you put that same level of thought into each outfit, you will get good results. Instead of diluting your attention among 90 separate outfits, focus on 1-3 outfits. You'll get them right. You might get some help from friends and family to do so. But when you perfect those outfits, you will always be at your best.

The Ashtray

Many years ago, the military was once again under scrutiny for wasting money. The media picked up on a particularly expensive ashtray used in submarines.

The ashtray was quite expensive because it had to break into no more than three pieces when struck with a hammer. Having a thousand shards of glass flying around a submarine was considered dangerous enough to warrant the expense.

The media jumped on these expensive ashtrays. They pointed out that metal ashtrays could do the same at a fraction of the cost. They also pointed out that smoking was not even allowed on the submarines, so the ashtrays had questionable appropriateness in the first place.

While in that particular situation those ashtrays may have been silly, they actually serve as a positive example for how to think about objects. Clearly, whoever had those ashtrays requisitioned put a lot of thought into them. They hadn't just bought the first thing that came to mind. They put time and consideration into the purchase.

That represents the kind of thought that can take Materialistic Minimalism to its highest levels, and take you to your highest level. When you think carefully before you buy things, when you consider each purchase deeply, you end up with things provide the greatest enhancements to your life. When you make sure that everything you buy passes the three checks, fits your color palette, and is has been carefully considered, you can get the most out of the material part of your life.

CHAPTER 12:

Impulse Purchases

Can you still make impulse purchases while practicing Materialistic Minimalism?

Not really.

Technically, you can see if something passes the Three Checks pretty quickly. But your goal is not to buy every single thing on earth that passes the Three Checks. Millions of things do.

Materialistic Minimalism, at its heart, is about only buying the things that enhance your life the most. Over time, you should end up with fewer and better things.

Q: But I love impulse purchases! It's fun.

A: By definition, an impulse is a desire. Giving in to a desire will generally be pleasant.

However, impulses are generally irrational desires. Giving in to them does not improve your life.

As adults, we have become so good at controlling our desires that we don't often realize that we are doing it. But consider for a moment how good you are at controlling your impulses.

You routinely walk by candy displays without buying candy. When you are angry, you don't scream or punch people. Even if you would rather sit around and eat marshmallows, you may exercise or eat food with some nutritional value.

If you started giving in to your impulses, your life would get a lot worse. Within a few days, you could make yourself sick or lethargic, or get yourself fired or thrown in jail.

Just as impulsively giving in to candy or violence isn't particularly beneficial, giving in to impulse purchases is counterproductive. But, it's really hard to resist impulse purchases. Sure, if you are going to your local grocery store, you can easily resist impulse purchases. But what if there's a huge sale? What if your favorite store releases a new line of clothing or watches or shoes?

And things get more dangerous when you're on vacation. You see a fridge magnet, silly t-shirt, or other bit of foolishness designed to separate tourists from their money. You're relaxed. You're on vacation. You've bent the rules of your diet a bit. Why not?

You are just buying clutter. And unlike the 2-3 pounds you gain on vacation, it may take years to get rid of that stupid fridge magnet or pointless doodad.

And please don't fall into that trap of, "Buy it here because it's cheaper." Tourist areas are always targeted by scam artists. For example, one of the largest markets for fake rubies is at the famous real ruby mines in Burma. Scam artists know that people expect to be able to buy rubies more cheaply near the source. They target unsuspecting tourists, who assume that the only rubies so close to the mines will be real. Of course, scam artists just bring fake rubies with them.

A general rule of thumb: never buy anything when you travel, ever. Even when you are travelling to a poor country where you expect to get good deals, remember that often countries are poor because of cultures of dishonesty. Companies cannot do business there, since no one can be trusted. Many friends and family, hoping to save a few dollars, have ended up buying fake or worthless items in China, India, Cambodia, Argentina, and other parts of Asia and South America.

This is especially true in seemingly authentic side of the road bazaars. Those bazaars are specifically designed to manipulate the stereotypical expectations of Western Tourists.

Furthermore, fashions in many parts of the third world are less sophisticated. While a custom-made suit may look good in another part of the world, when compared with a designed suit in America, it will look unpolished.

Clothes that look good in poor countries will just look poor in rich countries.

There are two situations in which it's generally okay to buy things while on vacation.

First, if the entire purpose of the trip was to buy something, then you can buy that thing. For example, "I want to go to the Vallée de Joux to buy this specific Patek Philippe Watch." This is not the same as wanting to buy just any old Patek Philippe watch, which you can do in pretty much any major American city for the same price. It only makes sense if this particular watch can't be bought elsewhere.

Second, if there is something very specific, created by a specific person, available in only one country, you can buy that thing on a vacation there. One of my few non-donated possessions was created by Marcelo Toledo, a famous Argentine silversmith. But it wasn't particularly cheap to buy it in his workshop in Argentina. I would have paid the same buying it in his online store. Being there just allowed me to see the item before I bought it, and make a more informed decision.

That is very different from buying some random piece of side of the road Argentine silver jewelry, much of which is fake, and none of which is cheaper than what you would pay in America. The price of silver, gold, platinum, and precious stones is the same worldwide. If you think you are getting a deal in some third world tourist area, chances are you are getting a fake.

There is technically a third type of overseas purchase that makes logical sense, which is if you intend to buy something that is just illegal in your home country. Unless you are an arms dealer or a human trafficker, this probably does not apply to you.

Don't buy spices, clothes, or jewelry overseas. Trust me: when you compare the spices you buy in Southeast Asia to the spices that professional spice buyers at Whole Foods buy in Southeast Asia, you'll see that the professionals do it better. When you compare the clothes from South America to the ones professional buyers source from South America, you'll see the difference. With modern transportation and shipping, you don't need to be Marco Polo or Christopher Columbus to get nice things from other countries. Just buy them, if and when you need them, at a local store or online retailer.

Sales

Sales are intentionally designed to encourage impulse purchases. "40 percent off today only buy right now this second or else" doesn't really give you much time to think. What do you do?

Ask yourself this: were you already planning to buy that item? Had you previously considered the item, thought about it carefully, and decided to buy it? And now that it is on sale it seems to be a good time to buy? If so, sure, go ahead.

But if you just want to buy it because it is on sale, don't. If it's something that you had not ever thought about, but it seems like a good deal, do not buy it.

Remember, as a Materialistic Minimalist, you can afford to spend a lot more per item than mass consumers. Because you have far fewer items than mass consumers, you can spend more per item. A 50% off sale doesn't make any difference. Only purchase things you have carefully considered.

More importantly, the only things that ever go on huge sales are things that were heavily marked up in the first place. Businesses that price their products based on the actual value of those products usually deal in things of higher value. Businesses that charge people different prices for the same goods, based on what the individual consumer is willing to pay, generally sell lower quality goods. Avoiding businesses that use huge sale gimmicks is a pretty good general rule.

Materialistic Minimalism and Finances

Materialistic Minimalism done right will save money and improve your life. If done recklessly, it can make you go broke.

It can be tempting to slip into a mindset of "I must have the best of everything no matter what the cost." That's not Materialistic Minimalism. That's lunacy. If you want the best car on earth, the best clothes on earth, the best watch on earth, the cost will be astronomical. Whatever tranquility you gain from Minimalism will be more than cancelled out by massive financial pressure.

Here are a few rules of thumb.

1. Before you buy anything new, first maximize what you already have. You might not need to buy a single new thing. You may well be able to improve your life solely by donating things.

2. Materialistic Minimalism should cost less, not more. While each thing you buy may cost more, you should be buying far fewer things. The total cost should be lower.

3. Do not debt-finance your Materialistic Minimalism.

If you don't have money for a new jacket, then wait until you do. Being a Materialistic Minimalist is not the same as being a spendthrift.

Be calm, smart, and careful. Materialistic Minimalism should improve your financial situation, not worsen it.

CHAPTER 13:

Kids and Grandkids

I have worked with many people who were saving items for their grandkids. These were not platinum heirlooms, but stuffed animals, kids' books, games, etc. These items often take up a lot of space, particularly in a small, studio apartment.

Why were these old men and women living in studio apartments? Because they were not old; they were in their early twenties. They didn't have grandkids. They didn't even have kids. They didn't even have people with whom they intended to procreate!

Many of us treasure parts of our childhoods, and naturally want to pass that feeling of wonder to our descendants. We try to do so by passing down the same physical objects that brought us that feeling.

Unfortunately, your descendants will likely have very different preferences than you had as a child. They might find your treasured books old fashioned and weird. For idiosyncratic reasons, they might find your stuffed bear terrifying. Each child is different.

My dad loves books about hunting and adventure. He absolutely detests science fiction and fantasy books. I am the exact opposite. I love fantasy books, and find books about hunting uninteresting. It would make no sense for him to save books for me – and we actually have a pretty decent number of preferences in common! I can't imagine connecting with my grandfather's childhood books. They'd be written in a language that I cannot read, and they would come from a culture that is not part of my upbringing.

Toys from several generations in the past can seem quaint or historic. But they aren't usually seen as fun.

Furthermore, if you save a lot of stuff for your grandkids, you could decrease your probability of having grandkids in the first place. Such a high level of hoarding creates constant stress. The clutter makes people feel uncomfortable and irritated. The constant strain makes early divorce more likely.

Calm tranquility in the home will bring far more joy than crammed clutter.

Instead of saving these items for your great grandkids, consider giving them to someone else's existent grandkids. A child today is far more likely to appreciate those toys than a child 60 years from now. They are culturally closer, and will be able to connect more with the toys.

Then, when you do have kids or grandkids, you can be the cool grandparent. You can be the one that buys all the toys that the child likes, instead of giving them things that you like. You can get them the toys that they actually want, instead of burdening them with something from your completely different childhood.

Who knows what your grandkids will like? Will it be holographic toys? Or will things go retro, and will they want board games with wooden dice? Maybe your grandson will be a chess genius, and will want a new chess board. Maybe he will be an artist, and want a set of paints.

Don't save what is important to you. Try to discover what is important to them. Try to see your descendants for who they are, rather than just looking for your own reflected childhood. And save yourself the clutter in the process!

CHAPTER 14:

Sunk Costs

The first rule of economic investing: don't count your sunk costs. Don't say, "We already spent a billion dollars on this, so we have to continue." Instead look at the expected gains. Say, "If we spend an additional one billion dollars on this, will we get 2 billion dollars in expected returns?"

While investors know this, most other people do not. It's very counterintuitive. Once we have invested time and money into something, we feel obligated to continue that thing. We feel very guilty or foolish if we stop.

At the very least, when you shut down an investment, you have to admit that the investment was a waste of money. Psychologically, it is often easier to continue a losing investment than it is to admit that.

That's why one of the first rules of sales is to get people to invest! Salespeople try to get people to invest their time, or a little bit of money. Once a person has invested, they are more likely to continue investing, even if the benefits wane.

Political candidates get people to volunteer time or donate a small amount of money, realizing that those who do are more likely to follow up that behavior by voting and encouraging others to vote. Car salesmen get people to test drive a car, which involves putting in time. Colleges invite students on long and pointless tours, recognizing that those who invest time into a tour are more inclined to continue investing by attending the college. For that matter, colleges make long and burdensome applications for the same reason.

That's why it is often hardest to give away the things that create the biggest nuisances. It's not that hard to give away some mediocre pen you got for free at a trade show. You didn't invest anything in that.

It's much more emotionally difficult to donate a $2000 treadmill that you haven't ever used. You invested money into it. You spent time choosing it. You may have even put effort into assembling it. You have a lot of sunk costs.

When approaching sunk costs, you have two choices. Either approach the situation like a savvy investor. Or approach the situation like an incompetent investor.

Consider the treadmill example. Suppose you act like a savvy investor. You immediately sell the treadmill at a loss, or donate it if there are no easy buyers. The end result is you now have a whole section of a room, or even an entire room, available. You can use that room for something better than junk storage.

Now suppose you act like an incompetent investor. You can say, "Well, I spent so much on it, so I have to keep it. Even though it is just using up a room." Over time, since the foolish decision makes you feel guilty, you start to avoid the room with the treadmill. You only enter it to put some other unwanted object, and then quickly leave.

I cannot even begin to estimate the number of households in which "exercise room" just means junk room.

Savvy investors are not those who never make mistakes. Everyone on earth makes mistakes.

Savvy investors just don't compound their mistakes. They don't turn a level one mistake into a level ten mistake.

So, you made a stupid purchase. You know who else has done that? Everyone else on earth.

You don't owe it to anyone to make yourself unhappy forever. You don't have to rub your own nose in it. You don't have to sacrifice an entire room of your house to it.

You made a mistake. We all do. Admit it, get rid of it, and move on.

Try to make fewer mistakes in the future, but recognize that you will probably make at least one more mistake in your lifetime. Don't dwell on those mistakes. Don't sink into them. As soon as you realize you've made a mistake, fix it. Don't spend 10 years in denial first. When you buy something stupid, admit it, donate it, and move on.

Donating, Gifting, or Selling

When you have something large, expensive, and unwanted, it's hard to know what to do. Should you donate it? Give it as a gift? Sell it?

You may be thinking that selling it is the best option. It can be. But the problem is, selling things often involves a lot of procrastination.

I have found that creating a deadline works well for me and others I've helped through the process. I write a date on a piece of paper, and attach that paper to the item. Usually, that date is 1 week in the future. If I have not sold the item by then, I donate it.

You can make the date two weeks in the future. But don't make it two months in the future. That's silly.

The same system applies for gifts. If I think something will make a nice gift, I put a date on it. If I haven't given it to a specific person by then, I just donate it.

Some nicer things can be sold through consignment stores or pawn shops. With those, not only do you make money, you also get your space back. But if you plan to use those, make sure you put a date on the item to ensure you do, in fact, take it to the store. Don't let your Inner Hoarder trick you through procrastination!

The One Year Rule

One of my favorite rules is the one year rule. If I haven't used an item in a full year, I automatically donate it.

It's sometimes amazing to see how many things the one year rule eliminates. It also lets you see what you're keeping for actual use, compared to what you are keeping compulsively. And this rule is a great way to combat the guilty feelings of sunk costs.

The one year rule will help you get rid of some of your particularly pernicious items. These are items that you don't really want, but feel compelled to keep.

The most flagrant violators of the one year rule: expensive clothes, kitchen gadgets, and exercise equipment.

Most of us have at least one fancy clothing item that we have not worn in the last year. Sometimes, it's something that has never been worn at all.

When we buy those types of clothes, it's not in response to some immediate need. It's never, "I'm constantly going out to these fancy events where ball gowns/tuxedos with coattails are needed. But I don't have one, so I must buy this one."

Instead, we desire an alternative, more glamorous lifestyle, and we think, "If I buy this dress/tuxedo, I'll end up going to fancy outings all the time.

It's an easy trap to fall into.

The most reliable way to avoid falling into that trap is to only buy an item in response to a real need. Don't fall into the obviously illogical trap of assuming that the object will magically create its own need. Instead, work on the logical steps that actually lead to your goal.

As an illustration, an eighth grader who plans to become a doctor should not begin by purchasing an MRI machine. He should work on academics.

A person who wants to get married should not begin by purchasing a wedding dress or a tuxedo. That person might begin by setting up an online dating profile.

A person who wants to go to a nice event should first either buy tickets to an event, or network in order to get invited to private events.

Envisioning a goal can be beneficial, but that doesn't require cluttering your closet with unusable (or not yet useable) clothing. Some people like to use Pinterest boards. Others like to make digital lists of goals, and strategies on how to pursue them.

Don't be like an eighth grader who fills his house with expensive and large medical equipment, but forgets to do his homework. Focus on the actual steps to your goal.

And if you make a mistake by buying an expensive item of clothing, don't punish yourself forever for it. Donate it and move on.

Kitchen Devices

The same principle applies to kitchen devices. We imagine a different, self-sufficient gourmet life. In this imaginary world, we make our own bread, fresh juice, yogurt, etc. Drawn to the earthy glamor of that life, we buy all the equipment for it. We use it once or twice, and then stop. Then, feeling guilty for our irresponsible purchase or laziness, we let the device sit on the kitchen counter for years, turning a sunk cost into stressful kitchen clutter.

It's easy to know when it's time to get rid of a kitchen device: if you haven't used it for a year, donate it. If it's only been a month or two, but you almost definitely won't use it, donate it.

How do you know whether or not to buy a kitchen device? The two key points are need and current actions.

First, is there a pressing need? For example, do you

have an easy way to access bread? If so, you probably won't need or ever use a bread machine.

Second, how often do you currently do the task that the gadget is for? In other words, have you ever made bread by hand? Do you do it regularly? If so, a bread machine may make your life easier. On the other hand, if you have never made bread by hand, it is unlikely that a bread machine will ever get used.

New equipment almost never changes behavior. It can enhance existing behavior. But it is very unlikely that it will create new behavior.

People made bread for thousands of years before the first electronic bread maker. If you already make bread regularly, and feel like a bread maker will save you a few minutes a day, great. But do not expect a bread maker to cause you to start making bread. The guilt of buying an expensive machine often only convinces you to use that machine once or twice, if at all. And anyways, why buy something just to guilt yourself into doing a task? If you don't want to do something, don't do it. And don't buy expensive tools to help you not do it.

Exercise Equipment

As a quick glance at eBay will show you, there is a lot of unused exercise equipment out there. Most of it comes from the wrongheaded idea that fancy equipment will change behavior. But as we discussed with kitchen tools, fancy equipment only enhances existing behavior.

The rules for kitchen equipment apply to exercise equipment. If you use dumbbells at home already, you can upgrade those dumbbells and expect they will get used. If you are currently using an in-home treadmill, you will probably also use a fancier one, or some other large machine (like an elliptical or a bike).

If you're considering buying a large workout machine for the first time, though, what do you compare it to? Realistically, if you already jump rope or do workout videos at home consistently, then you might use an elliptical machine. If you already bike a lot on roads, then you might use an in-home bike.

But if you don't already exercise at home, new equipment won't change that. If you've never done a pushup at home, it is unlikely that you will use an expensive weight lifting apparatus. So, when considering your purchase, be sure that you are never buying anything because you "will do" something.

If you want to exercise at home, I recommend trying out P90X-3, or Insanity Max 30. These great workout programs require relatively little equipment. Insanity requires none. P90X requires a pullup bar, which can be wall mounted, and exercise bands, which cost around $15 and take up minimal space.

Work on changing your behavior first. Once you've established the right habits, and feel the need for better equipment, go for it. But don't expect equipment to change your habits. It will not.

And of course, anything you don't use within one year must be donated. That doesn't mean that at the end of one year you should use your elliptical one time, convince yourself you'll surely use it again, and then let it sit unused for another year. Using a large machine once a year is an enormous waste of space. In that case, just buy a guest pass at a gym one day a year.

CHAPTER 15:

Materialistic Minimalism for Millionaires

This chapter is for millionaires and people who plan to become millionaires.

Many of us fantasize about being wealthy. We say, if I become a millionaire, I'm going to get twenty sports cars, and thirty Rolexes, and a closet full of expensive clothes and shoes.

I've met quite a few people who did just that. I've seen fleets of sports cars, huge watch collections, massive shoe collections, and the like.

But as fancy as these collections were, frankly, they could have been a lot fancier.

In each of those situations, people substituted quantity for quality. Instead of getting one incredible thing, they settled for 50 lesser things.

This may sound shocking. How is a Rolex or a Ferrari lesser?

Rolexes and Ferraris are anything but mediocre. But they are also not the upper limit of materialism.

Instead of multiple Rolexes, a person can buy a single Patek Philippe watch. Unless you plan to wear thirty watches at a time like a mental patient, there's no real advantage to having so many watches. A person who can afford thirty Patek Philippe watches can consider a rare and exceptional Patek Philippe watch, or a custom made Vacheron Constantin Atelier Cabinotiers watch.

A person who can afford multiple Ferraris may consider a McLaren P1, a Bugatti Veyron, or just a higher end Ferrari.

A person who can afford fifty pairs of diamond earrings may consider an exceptional pair of red, green, or blue diamond earrings.

A person who can afford fifty Mont Blanc pens may consider a Graf von Faber Castell Pen of the Year.

No matter how high you go, you can always go higher. There is never a reason to go horizontal by just buying more of the same. There is always a next level.

Materialistic Minimalism Encourages Learning

Many readers may not have heard of some of the items mentioned in the previous section. That's another great thing about Materialistic Minimalism: it forces you to learn about materials and new items.

Since Materialistic Minimalists buy fewer items, we can spend more per item. We can also consider each purchase more carefully.

That means we have both the time and the impetus

to learn a lot more about each item before purchasing. While mass consumers purchase haphazardly, Materialistic Minimalists purchase very carefully.

We end up learning much more about each area. Some of the things mentioned in the previous section cost a lot. For example, a McLaren P1 costs well over a million dollars.

But other things don't cost that much. A bar of Amano chocolate costs less than $10. It's much more expensive than a Hershey bar, but it is also something truly exceptional.

Even when Materialistic Minimalists fantasize about being rich, they become more educated. They don't say, "If I had a million dollars, I would buy a million earrings." They say, if I had a million dollars to spend on a single pair of earrings, what would I buy? In that exploration, they learn about rare gemstones, historically significant jewelers, highly skilled methods of construction, etc.

Materialistic Minimalists often become connoisseurs of quality, rather than hoarders of quantity. In doing so, they become much more educated than mass consumers, and they gain access to the exceptional things available today.

In my own experience, I have learned about the existence of things that I could not have previously imagined. My desire to find things that follow the

Materials Check once brought me to Hearne Hardwoods, a store that sells exotic hardwoods. I found woods there beyond anything I have ever imagined. I saw purpleheart, a wood that is naturally purple, and tiger maple, which is iridescent. I learned about the majesty of English Elm, and the deep, fascinating beauty of quilted mahogany. Before Materialistic Minimalism, I would never have even considered that such things could exist, let alone had any reason to find them.

Many individuals have exceptional things hidden away in their closets, protected by a moat of mediocre things. The entire marketplace is like that as well. There are incredible things available in the world. They are hidden behind moats of hyped up mediocrity. But if you push past empty branding and massive advertising, you will discover a world of incredible treasures.

Labor and the Source of Value

It's no surprise that I disagree with the political views of Karl Marx, the intellectual father of modern communism. But you may be surprised to discover that I actually agree with some of his analysis of economics!

Marx explains that market value generally reflects

the amount of labor incorporated into a good. For example, a cup that takes 10 hours to make will probably cost about 10 times as much as a cup that takes 1 hour to make.

Gold costs more than aluminum because it takes so much labor to mine it. In the past, when aluminum was more difficult to extract, it used to cost a lot! There were even royal crowns made out of aluminum.

Natural gems are expensive because it takes so much time and labor to find one.

Generally, things that require very skilled labor cost more than things that require the same amount of unskilled labor.

Expensive things are generally things that require a lot of labor to create. Something made of gold begins at a higher price than something made of silver because it takes more labor to mine gold than to mine silver.

But when considering things of exceptional value, it is often wise to consider the labor input as a whole, rather than first focusing on the cost of materials. For example, the legendary Swiss watch company Audemars Piguet pointedly made the reference version of their million dollar grande complication watch in titanium, rather than platinum. They were letting buyers know that it was not the few hundred dollars' worth of platinum, but rather the thousands of hours of highly skilled labor, that made this watch exceptional.

The same is true of metalworking in general. Forging metal (beating it into a particular shape with a hammer) takes much more effort than lost wax casting. The metal is the same, but the labor involved is much greater when the metal is forged. Exceptional metalwork items are often forged. Because of the greater labor involved, the market value is higher.

Whether you are a millionaire or not yet there, learning about the world of exceptional products, and what makes them exceptional, can be fascinating. And it's a great reminder that you never need to substitute quantity for quality. There is always something better.

CHAPTER 16:
Gifts

Mass consumers love gifts. A gift is another thing to add to their pile of low grade stuff.

But Materialistic Minimalists often feel a bit differently. After all, their goal is to have fewer, nicer things, not more things. It's nice to be thought of, but a gift can become just another thing to deal with.

We often feel very guilty about donating our gifts. Someone took time to buy the gift. They spent money on it. If you just give it away, you feel rude and ungrateful.

It's a tricky situation to navigate.

The first step is to let your friends and family know that you are doing Materialistic Minimalism, and how excited you are to be donating so many things. Talk about how you are working to eliminate clutter, to empty your closets, to empty your cupboards, etc. Even if your friends and family don't know what Materialistic Minimalism is, they'll get the general idea that you don't want more things. This will make them less likely to give you things that you have to later feel guilty about donating.

What about distant relatives and acquaintances?

Pragmatically speaking, they don't see you often enough to know whether or not you donated the gift. Send a thank you note, and then donate the item.

For politeness, you can keep a gift for 24 hours. But that's as far as politeness needs to go. You don't owe it to anyone to decrease your standard of living for any reason.

Sentimental Gifts and Heirlooms

Some gifts have more sentimental value than others. Sometimes, we keep a gift because it reminds us of a relative who has passed away, or a close friend who is currently abroad.

Small tokens can make us feel connected to those we love. But it's important to remember that the valuable thing is the connection we feel to the person, not the physical token (unless the token does, in fact, have some inherent value).

It's also important to be intelligent about the numbers. If you keep a necklace to remind you of your great grandmother, that makes sense. The physical object can create a kind of sense memory that connects you to the person.

But if you need ten necklaces to remind you of your great grandmother, either she wasn't that memorable, or you aren't that bright. Having ten necklaces doesn't mean you love her ten times as much. It just means you have ten times as much clutter.

Of course, some heirlooms actually pass the standards of Materialistic Minimalism. Those are completely separate issues. Those don't count as sentimental keepsakes.

But you should do your best to limit the purely sentimental keepsakes. Those are the keepsakes that have only sentimental value, rather than regular value.

Sentimental keepsakes hit you where you are most emotionally vulnerable. You feel guilty about giving them away, and your Inner Hoarder capitalizes on that guilt. I've worked with people who have, for sentimental reasons, kept dozens of things from a parent – who is perfectly healthy and alive!

When we are kids, parents often heavily emphasize the importance of appreciating gifts. When we are very young, parents often remind us that they had to save money to buy a gift, so we should be very grateful. This is not surprising: young children often have young parents who are early in their careers, and just don't make very much money yet.

But it's not effective to let that childhood guilt rule our adult behavior. You own your own space. You choose what goes in it. You should choose based on an intelligent system of values, not based on childhood guilt.

My general rule of thumb: I will keep up to one sentimental gift per person. I won't keep two sentimental gifts from anyone.

One interesting, relating category of stuff is birthday cards and other greeting cards. It can feel weird to throw them away, and there would be no point in donating them. I think the best solution is to take a cell phone picture of the ones you like the most, and then throw all of them out.

CHAPTER 17:

The Ferrari Principle

The inside of a Ferrari is magnificent. It's as precise and perfect as a swiss watch. Each part of the space is used intelligently. Whatever can be done to reduce weight is done.

Every so often, Ferrari comes out with a new engine for its elite models.

Here's what they don't do: they don't keep the old engine and then also add the new engine. That would transform an engineering work of art into a bizarre monstrosity.

Once they have something better, they use the better thing. They don't keep everything.

You can run your life in the same way. When you get something better, get rid of the old thing. Even if the old thing is nice, just keep the nicest thing. The old thing can be someone else's nicest thing.

This is one of the hardest parts of materialistic minimalism. It's not that hard to donate your tenth-rate things. It can be really hard to donate your second-best thing. But doing so brings you to a whole new level of strength, calm, and excellence.

Backups

Your second-best things should not be kept as backups. There are not many areas of our personal lives that tend to require backups at all.

Sometimes, it makes sense to have backups in business. In my education business, we have a backup printer. This makes sense, because of the high-speed nature of the work. If our one and only printer fails, we could have a major problem. So instead, we have an extra printer to alleviate the potential for that problem.

Movie studios have all kinds of backups. They have backup cameras, lights, extension cords, microphones, etc. After all, if a camera fails during a shoot with highly paid actors and expensive, rented sets, that could be a financial catastrophe.

In many high-pressure, time sensitive situations, you need to have backup equipment. But for most things in your life, you don't need backups.

Rings rarely fail. They have no moving parts at all, and they're made of strong materials. An earring could break, but if it does, it's not vital equipment. Even the Queen of England or a famous actress can go for a day without earrings.

Those of us who work in very demanding professional environments in which backup equipment is the norm often erroneously use the same principle where it makes much less sense. A Hollywood photo shoot should have 20-30 extra extension cords. But in your house, you probably don't need that.

As you get closer to the ideal level of Materialistic Minimalism, find and donate backups. Get rid of the spare cords, the spare parts, and the backup equipment. Just keep what you need. If something fails, just buy a better one then. Given the speed of technological advancement, by the time the original piece of equipment fails, there may be a better option available!

CHAPTER 18:
Two Extreme Examples

You know about my journey through Materialistic Minimalism. Most people's journeys have been pretty similar. But there are two examples that have stood out that I think are worth telling. One involved a doctor; the other involved a fashion enthusiast.

Situation 1: Doctor Doing Locums

A doctor friend of mine does locums. That means he does short term contracts at hospitals that have a doctor shortage. He goes from one city to another.

He is also a motorcycle enthusiast. He decided he wanted to limit himself to just what he could keep in his motorcycle saddlebags. The total storage space is roughly equivalent to a medium sized camping bag.

Instead of having a small number of things, he had almost zero things. The few things he had were of the highest quality, and he used them for everything. He has motorcycle boots that are nice enough to wear to work and to go out. His jacket is versatile enough for any circumstance. His laptop is small, light and powerful.

If something breaks or wears out, he just buys a new one.

He is able to travel anywhere at a moment's notice. He is completely free and always ready for any situation. By limiting his possessions to such a small space, he forces himself to only use the best, and gives himself a level of freedom few of us can even dream about.

Situation 2: Fashion Enthusiast on Vacation

The second situation involves a fashion enthusiast on vacation. A friend of mine has a huge collection of clothes. Today that collection is about 90 percent smaller, but even now, you could say she is in an early phase of Materialistic Minimalism, at best.

Although she has a large collection of clothing, and an impeccable sense of fashion, she often just wears the same mediocre sweat clothes repeatedly. Her arguments are all the same as we've seen thus far: convenience, comfort, and saving her fancier things for special occasions.

But last year, she inadvertently took Materialistic Minimalism to a really high level. She had planned a three week long trip through southeast Asia and could only take a single large camping backpack. She also likes taking photographs, so she wanted to make sure she would look her best. She decided to plan each outfit, instead of just picking clothes at random.

When she came back, she was extremely excited. During the entire trip, she had felt like a famous actress or princess. She had no choice but to dress well, since all of her frumpy sweats were left at home. Every day, she looked her best. The homely clothes had been replaced by her nice, fashionable clothes. She didn't have to buy new clothes, she just made use of the ones she had.

She has already donated many, many bags of clothes. Those who receive them are always excited, as she does have an impressive fashion sense. But she has benefitted the most, since she now defaults to her nicer clothes instead of her ill-fitting, unflattering clothes.

CHAPTER 19:

Materialistic Minimalism and Food

Our compulsions come from millennia of culture, and an even longer genetic memory. The number one concern that humans had for most of our history was running out of food.

That deep compulsion guides us to buy and store food. Advertisers manipulate this desire and further encourage food hoarding.

The result is that we often have food stored up in our pantries that is over a year old. It's either spoiled, or originally made with so many preservatives that it was never worth eating.

Our refrigerators are jammed with food for all kinds of unlikely contingencies. As if constantly worried about a natural disaster that isolates us from all sources of food for several years, we hoard up food, wait for it to go bad, and then hoard up more food.

This habit is expensive, messy, and unhealthy. It also encourages us to buy second rate food, because it has more preservatives and therefore a longer shelf life.

Because we buy ten times as much food as we need, we must spend very little per item. Instead of buying a small, usable quantity of high quality food, we buy a massive amount of mediocre, unhealthy food.

The good news is that Materialistic Minimalism can help with food quality as well.

The steps are very similar. In the first phase, get rid of all the tenth-rate food. All the junk food with zero nutritional value has no place in your house. Then, start to get rid of all the second-rate food that's cluttering your house and harming your health. To help with that process, we can apply the three checks to food.

The Three Checks...For Food!

With other things, you have the Materials Check, the Engineering Check, and the Aesthetic Check. With food, you have the Ingredients Check, the Nutrition Check, and the Taste Check.

The first check is the Ingredients Check. Is this food made with proper ingredients? Or is it full of low grade substitutes like high fructose corn syrup?

Like the materials check, the ingredients check helps you determine the quality of the food. All food manufacturers will say that their food is the best and highest quality. But examining the ingredients will let you know if they were actually trying to make the best food they can make, or just trying to cut their costs to profit at your expense.

For example, high fructose corn syrup is cheaper than sugar. Thus, when you see it used, you know the manufacturer is not really concerned with quality, but rather with making an easy profit.

It can take some time to learn what good ingredients look like. Food manufacturers have been tricking consumers for decades. They are pretty good at it.

I recommend looking at some Paleo diet sites to get started. Paleo dieters really emphasize simple, natural ingredients.

But honestly, a lot of it isn't that hard. If you buy maple syrup and the only ingredient is Grade A Maple Syrup, it's probably pretty decent. If instead it has 90 ingredients with complex chemical names you can't pronounce, it doesn't pass the Ingredients Check.

If it says, "Tastes like real __________." and it's half the cost, that's something to stay away from. As a simple example: Aunt Jemima's "Pancake Syrup" has nothing to do with actual maple syrup.

One ingredient to look out for is vanillin. Real vanilla comes from vanilla beans, part of the vanilla orchid. It is an expensive, high quality ingredient that has many chemical components. Vanillin, on the other hand, is a byproduct of industrial paper processing. It is a cheaper substitute to true vanilla. When you see "vanillin," you know you are dealing with a lower quality product, even if that product is expensive.

I was shocked to discover that Godiva uses vanillin, rather than real vanilla, in their truffles. That discovery made me stop buying Godiva. That, in turn, caused me to discover far superior alternatives from Teuscher, Amedei, Valrhona, Michel Cluizel, Amano, Knipschildt, and others. Instead of blindly following Godiva's branding, I independently learned about far superior alternatives.

The second check is the Nutrition Check. Something can be made of only natural ingredients, and have no protein, for example. Make sure what you eat has the protein and vitamins that will benefit your health.

While well-made chocolates may still have some sugar, those are eaten in moderation. The more problematic source of sugar in most diets is found everywhere else. Sugar these days is added to many sauces on meats and vegetables, and to frozen foods and dressings. These things may have "real, raw sugar," but they still show poor craftsmanship. It may make sense to add sugar to candies, but there is no real need for sugar in savory foods.

Note that food manufacturers have many ways to trick consumers into not seeing the sugar in the ingredients. They come up with all kinds of preposterous names. Evaporated cane juice just means sugar. Maltodextrin is just a type of sugar. Juice concentrates are also basically just sugar.

Learning about these damaging ingredients is an ongoing process. If you're not sure about an ingredient, just look it up. Before too long, you'll know which ingredients to avoid. As food manufacturers come up with new names for damaging ingredients (for example, calling sugar "evaporated cane juice", "sucrose", or "glucose-fructose dimers") you'll easily keep up.

You'll also find brands that you can trust, who refuse to use damaging ingredients. This will help you avoid long grocery trips, and still stay healthy.

For any unhealthy food on the market, there is almost certainly a healthier version. In fact, there is a growing number of businesses that specialize in making healthy food that tastes good. These businesses use alternative ingredients that have more nutritional value. While they may cost a bit more, remember that you are no longer buying food to stuff into your kitchen. You are only buying the food that you will eat.

Finally, there is the Taste Check.

You've already discovered that clothes can be attractive and convenient. Similarly, food can be healthy and tasty. It often requires quite a bit of innovation to make that happen. Sometimes, that adds to the cost. But as a Materialistic Minimalist, you just buy food you actually plan to eat. Your goal is not to cram your kitchen with stuff you'll never even consider eating.

Because you buy fewer things, you can afford to spend a bit more per item. Instead of buying 90 packs of frozen vegetables you'll never eat, buy a small amount of fresh vegetables that you will eat. You should do the same with fruit.

I have always been a picky eater. But I also like to be healthy. Over the years, I have done all kinds of experiments to find ways to make healthy foods taste good. In fact, I've even found ways to like some of my previously least favorite foods, by using the right mix of spices or other ingredients.

McDonalds can take low grade garbage meat and make it taste good. If you experiment, you can almost certainly do the same with high quality, healthy ingredients!

CHAPTER 20:
The Small and Overlooked

Keychains

Keychains are junk magnets. A keychain ornament is a small purchase, so we often buy keychains when we travel. It's an easy gift, so friends often give us keychains. Over time, keychains expand.

This creates a big, heavy nuisance you need to carry. Often, keychains get so big that people need to carry purses or backpacks just to store the metal monsters. Once we have the bag, it's easy to fill the bag with even more needless stuff.

My rule for keychains: a keychain should only have the keys you use daily. Not the backup security outdoor fence key. Just the front door key, car key, and that's it.

It should have between 0 and 1 ornaments. Instead of having 20 average ornaments, just get one exceptional ornament. Make sure it passes the three checks.

It should have one ring, not 15 interlocking rings.

One ring, 2-3 keys, and at most one ornament.

It may take a few hours to cull your keychain down. That's no big deal. It took me a few weeks! Be patient with yourself, and you'll get there.

Wallets

Wallets, like keychains, collect all kinds of randomness. Instead of being simple and convenient, wallets often become massive and burdensome.

Today, this problem is worse than ever. Restaurants and grocery stores love to advertise in your wallet. They give you discounts if you carry their card around with you. Restaurants give you cards that they stamp that will give you a free sandwich in 6 months. Grocery stores will give you 5 cents off of a gallon of milk. While we don't want to carry the stupid card around, we feel guilty about not saving money. Many of us carry a dozen grocery store and restaurant cards, and several credit cards. Once we have so much garbage, we start adding other people's business cards, receipts, and all kinds of other randomness.

Eventually, there are so many cards that we often forget to use them at the stores they're intended for. Or we spend so long trying to locate the card in our wallets that customers behind us become irritated and we start to feel guilty. Often, we just give up, pay the full price, and leave without ever finding the right discount card, coupon, or frequent visitor card.

Most people would prefer a clean, light, simple wallet. But how do we get there? Different credit cards give us different advantages. Different stores give us different discounts. We need the cards!

Let's tackle this one at a time. You need one credit card. Not 60. Find a VISA or MasterCard that you like, that gives you whatever benefits you value, and then get rid of the rest. Yes, you might lose out on a 2% discount at one particular restaurant in some random state. Is that $5 worth turning your wallet into a trash bucket for life?

For grocery store cards: you don't need them. In every grocery store or convenience store, you have the option of using your phone number if you don't have your card. As soon as you fill out the card information, throw away the physical card. Only use your phone number. This statement is also true for those keychain cards. Every single keychain access card you have should be removed and thrown out. You can almost always use your cell phone number, and when you can't, it's just not worth it.

For restaurant cards: go without them. You will end up spending an extra $8 per year. That's paying for comfort and convenience. You probably pay more than $8 extra per year for your house or apartment, compared to a studio in a less desirable part of town. We pay for quality of life.

Many restaurants, realizing that people don't want to carry around junk, have started using smartphone apps instead. Those are ideal alternatives, since they take no physical space and still give you the free cup of coffee every 30 weeks.

The best investment I ever made: I donated my large, jammed, clunky wallet, and replaced it with a slim, credit card wallet. It has room for a bit of cash, a driver's license, a debit card, a health insurance card. It's nice, convenient, small, and lightweight.

Other Materialistic Minimalists have taken it even further! They use credit card wallets that attach easily to the back of their cell phones. They have eliminated the wallet entirely, and created a whole new level of minimalist, streamlined, convenience.

Buy an E-reader

It took me a long time to even try an e-reader. I hate reading on computer screens, so I figured I would also hate reading on an e-reader. To my surprise, an e-reader is nothing like a computer screen. E-readers don't use bright backlights like computer screens, so it feels more like looking at ink on a page.

Some e-readers today use backlights, like the Kindle Paperwhite. I personally prefer to turn that backlight off. I spend all day looking at a computer screen, which is pretty much the same as staring at a light bulb.

But whether you keep the backlight on or off, an

e-reader is a small purchase that can massively help you declutter your house. You can get rid of the physical books that take up space, and have more space and tranquility.

With an e-reader, you also never have to hunt for a book. The device will find it for you. When you travel, you don't have to weigh yourself down with books. Keep your bags light, and keep as many books at your fingertips as you can possibly hope to read.

I know that many people love the smell of books. But using that as a reason to avoid e-readers is like allowing the "new car smell" to be a reason to avoid buying a jet, teleporter, or time machine. Kindles smell different, but their advantages are so massive that they more than make up for it. And anyways, the "musty smell of books" is just mold and mildew.

CHAPTER 21:
Materialistic Minimalism
for Your House

Size vs. Location

With a house, you pay for two things: size and location. Convenience and desirability of location tends to matter more. A one bedroom apartment in Manhattan, for example, costs more than a ten bedroom house in Montana.

If you have a ten bedroom house when you only need two bedrooms, you're wasting money. If you have 8 of those bedrooms full of nonsense, you are paying a high premium for junk storage, when you could be spending that same money on a better location. You could move to a better part of whatever city you live in. Or you could move to a better city. Or, if city life isn't for you, you could find a better location away from the city.

Here, as elsewhere, there is always a next level. Don't waste your money on useless space and junk storage when you could have the convenience of a better location.

The Dining Room

It's a bit silly to have an expensive shirt that you wear only once a year. But it is downright insane to do the same with an expensive room.

Many people have a formal dining room. It's often the nicest room in the house, and usually quite conveniently located right next to the kitchen. And it is often left completely unused.

If you have a dining room, you are paying for it. You are paying a higher mortgage for it. You are giving up a better location without a dining room in order to have a house with a dining room. It is a financial cost, and an opportunity cost.

Like nice silverware or clothes, a dining room should be used daily, not wasted.

Lessons of Fallingwater

One of the architectural marvels of the world is Fallingwater, built by legendary architect Frank Lloyd Wright. Wright understood the importance of Materialistic Minimalism, although he didn't use that phrase. Much of the architectural decisions are designed to specifically encourage Materialistic Minimalism.

If you've never seen a picture, take a look at one online. From the outside, it is majestic and breathtaking. On the inside, it is a pure expression of architectural brilliance.

But it is not big. It's around 3000 square feet. That's comfortable, but much smaller than the average McMansion.

Wright built Fallingwater as a peaceful getaway for the client. He knew that clutter was the enemy of peace, so he made several key decisions to encourage minimalism. The first was making the house relatively small, in order to prevent storage of junk.

He also refused to put doors on the garages. He knew that a garage without a door would be used only to park cars. A garage with a door would be used to store stuff.

He made the desks very small: enough space to work, but not enough space to make a mess.

The client wanted a bigger desk in his room. Wright considered the desk to be large enough. Only when the client indicated that the desk was "Too small even to write a check to an architect," did he concede, and double the size. But even then, the double sized desk is much smaller than most desks. The other desks are, by most standards, tiny. But they are actually perfectly suited to work, and entirely unsuited to clutter.

Fallingwater exudes a sense of peace and tranquility, largely because it essentially forces Materialistic Minimalism.

Storage Space

Following the great ideas of Frank Lloyd Wright, you can eliminate your storage space and make your home more minimalistic by default.

Once you've emptied out a bookshelf, donate the bookshelf. Make it impossible for yourself to buy more things. If you clean out a storage dresser in your closet, immediately donate the dresser so that you can never store so much stuff again.

Many Materialistic Minimalists do this will shelves in their cupboards. These are very easy to remove, and make it impossible to buy ten different sets of cups or bowls, or to cram your pantry with junk.

Physically removing storage space puts you miles ahead of your Inner Hoarder. Without the shelves, it's harder for the Inner Hoarder to store needless, unused stuff.

Spare Rooms, Guest Rooms, Etc.

When buying or renting a home, there's often a trade off between size and location. A smaller home in a more desirable location has obvious advantages. It's closer to everything. You can walk to restaurants or stores (or to a waterfall, if you prefer a location in nature).

But the larger home has one advantage: it's easier to house overnight guests. It's easier to have your friends, in-laws, or extended family stay over.

Some readers are already sold on the smaller house. The last thing those readers want is in-laws visiting, or the annoying friends of their spouses. But others like having family around. Or, perhaps, they like throwing large, multi-room parties. Thus, they pay to have extra rooms, which they only use 4-6 times a year (if that).

Instead of paying for those unused rooms every day, you can buy a smaller, more conveniently located house, and rent rooms when you need them. For a tenth of the cost of an overlarge house, you can put your family in a 5-star hotel suite when they come to visit. You can rent out restaurants, bars, or dedicated party spaces for large parties when you have them... all for much less than the hundreds of square feet you're not using and paying for.

That also ensures that you only host the people you want. If you have spare rooms, you'll either be constantly saying no to tenth cousins and friends of friends...or just grudgingly hosting them.

A smaller house or apartment remains your space, untroubled by unwanted visitors. And you can always rent rooms for welcome visitors when you need them.

Do Not Buy a Summer Home

Of the many mistakes I have seen wealthy people make, one of the biggest is buying a summer home.

A summer home just steals vacations. You feel obligated to go there for every vacation. You paid so much for it; you can't just let it go to waste.

Wealthy people without summer homes travel the world. They explore one amazing city after another, enjoying the nuances of different five and six star hotels.

Wealthy people with summer homes just commute. They go from one home to the other.

There are times when having a second home makes sense. If you have a work schedule that allows you to spend half of your time in a different location, and would like a permanent setup there, that makes sense.

But a second home used exclusively for vacations will only steal your chance to explore the world, or reduce the funds available for better hotels when you do travel elsewhere.

BONUS:
Extending Materialistic Minimalism

The conflict between minimalism and hoarding doesn't stop at things. If you look carefully, you can see it in a few other locations too. In this bonus chapter I will discuss two areas: law and education.

Minimalism and Education

As of this writing, a major educational debate is happening surrounding Common Core, a method of teaching math. Most teachers and math experts hate it. The creators and financial beneficiaries of Common Core, not surprisingly, love it.

Common Core looks a lot like hoarding applied to math. For example, instead of teaching the one best method for multiplication, common core teaches every conceivable method. The same is true of division, and even addition and subtraction.

The result is mental clutter. Students can't remember any one technique, and they're never sure which technique to use. They pick random parts of different techniques and try to throw them together.

In my own education business, we fix that situation by applying educational minimalism. We make sure that each student knows only the most effective multiplication techniques. We encourage students to drop second rate techniques, just as I hope you will get rid of your second-rate things.

And as a result, our students thrive. They become valedictorians in their schools, go on to attend prestigious universities, and they learn faster and retain more information than their peers. Even students who struggle in school have transformed into successful, competitive students, just by embracing minimalism in education.

Minimalism and the Law

What would happen if lawmakers turned into hoarders? What if they kept every single law, long after it was needed? What if they kept laws that didn't really do anything, but only created clutter and nuisances? What if they added laws haphazardly, like shopping addicts manically adding clothes to their closets?

You don't have to imagine it. It's already here. There are literally hundreds of thousands of laws and regulations. The number is so high that all attempts to just count them have been unsuccessful as of this writing.

There are so many, that even big companies with legal teams cannot avoid breaking them. In *Three Felonies A Day*, Harvey Silvergate discusses how even well intentioned doctors and banks cannot manage to avoid violating laws. As the title suggests, since different laws have conflicting directives, even decent people end up violating three of them a day!

Some have suggested that the right approach is to start by tossing out at least two laws for each new law passed. Others have suggested freezing the number of laws, preventing the addition of any new ones, until the total number of laws is below 100.

Others suggest a reverse approach. They suggest throwing out all laws, starting with the Constitution, and then adding just the ones deemed necessary.

I think all of these suggestions have merit. I think that if we can turn our lawmakers from legal hoarders to legal minimalists, we'd all be much better off.

Conclusion

Materialistic Minimalism will be an ongoing process. You'll make mistakes. Maybe you'll be tempted into an impulse purchase. Maybe you'll forget to follow the Three Checks one time.

That's no big deal. Even today, I often make mistakes. Materialistic Minimalism is never easy. The psychological compulsions are a constant battle.

But when you make a mistake, don't beat yourself up. Correct the mistake and move forward.

Remember, you are fighting the strongest compulsions in the human psyche. But if you keep persevering, I believe you'll become even stronger.

About the Author

Arvin Vohra is a national political and educational commentator, as well as the creator of the philosophy of Materialistic Minimalism. He has appeared on MS-NBC, FOX, CBS, RT, and many major radio programs.

He is also the founder of Vohra Method, an educational company that focuses on online tutoring. His other books include *The Equation for Excellence: How to Make Your Child Excel at Math.*